Cornwall Revisited

"Hudson Highlands Under Snow" by the well-known artist Harry Wickey (1892-1968)
who made his home in Cornwall for over forty years.
Courtesy of Janet Dempsey.

CR

Other Works:

18th Century Homes in New Windsor (N.Y.) and its Vicinity
(1968, with Marian M. Mailler)

Washington's Lost Encampment
(1987)

Cornwall, N.Y.: Images from the Past
(1988, with Collette C. Fulton and James I. O'Neill)

Cornwall Revisited

❧

A Hudson River Community

Janet Dempsey

Janet Dempsey

Library Research Associates Inc.
Monroe, N.Y.
1997

Library Research Associates, Inc.
474 Dunderberg Road
Monroe, New York 10950

Library of Congress Cataloging-in-Publication Data:

Dempsey, Janet, 1921-
    Cornwall Revisited: A Hudson River Community / Janet Dempsey
    93p.
    Includes bibliographical references and index.
    ISBN:0-912526-79-3
    1. Cornwall (N.Y.)—History—Anecdotes.   I. Title.
F129.C82D46   1997   97-16916
974.7'31—dc21   CIP

CR

To all the people who have asked
to have my newspaper articles
collected into a book.

Table of Contents

CR

FOREWORD

The 18th century poet William Blake wrote of seeing a world in a grain of sand, and in a way that describes Janet Dempsey's new collection of essays concerning the town of Cornwall, New York. For many of the topics she chooses — from World War I and women's suffrage, to the advent of the automobile and motion pictures — have a universality that not only appeals to more than a local audience, but seems to gain clarity through the focus on a single small community.

Admittedly, Cornwall is not just an old burg. Picturesquely nestled at the northern foot of Storm King Mountain on the west shore of the Hudson River, its location a scant 40 miles from New York City helped to make it an important commercial port in the 18th and 19th centuries, while its spectacular scenery inspired artists and authors alike. Among the latter was Nathaniel Parker Willis, who came for a summer vacation in 1851 and liked it so much he lived there for the rest of his life, in the meantime making Cornwall familiar to readers everywhere through his books and articles.

In this day and age, it is Janet Dempsey who is sharing an equally strong love of Cornwall by preserving its rich history in print. But unlike Willis, who at times could be a tad turgid, Dempsey writes with a trenchant, "cut-to-the-chase" style that must come from her long career as a schoolteacher; a style further honed by her post-retirement commitment to writing a weekly history column for the local newspaper.

This avoidance of verbiage doesn't result in dried-up prose or a lack of detail, however. Dempsey is well aware of how the odd fact — such as the way a World War I cannon wound up near the Cornwall Town Hall — can enliven a sketch. Or she will add some obscure aspect of a well-known event, as when she comments on the conservation of grain supplies making Prohibition a patriotic issue. Readers will also applaud the way she keys the past into the present, particularly in the case of property, where the location or current name of an old estate will be thoughtfully included.

Throughout it all there runs an infectious thread of enthusiasm that is not surprising to those of us who are acquainted with the author. As Cornwall Town Historian, she has consistently made herself available to other researchers, wholeheartedly joining in the quest for information, and always sharing it with unselfish delight.

So long as there are people like Janet Dempsey, the preservation of our heritage is safe — something readily seen in this highly readable local history that also offers societal insights well beyond the town's boundaries.

Patricia Edward Clyne
August 1997

PREFACE

This book is dedicated to all the people who have stopped me on the street or in the grocery store with the query: "Why don't you collect your newspaper articles into a book?" I have, and here is Volume I — forty-seven articles selected from the two hundred and forty-seven which have appeared in *The Cornwall Local* since 1991.

These articles are an outgrowth of a project started over a decade ago — that of indexing the old Cornwall Locals — ten hours a week which finds me happily immersed in the mores of a Cornwall outwardly so different from the modern community. The index, housed in the Cornwall Public Library, constitutes a history in itself — the citizens, institutions, problems and growth of the town — a valuable tool for the researcher.

The choice of articles has been difficult. To avoid duplication with "Images From the Past", a pictorial history of Cornwall published by The Friends of the Cornwall Public Library in 1989, I decided to begin with the 1890s and focus attention on the first three decades of the present century. Although some events are mentioned in both books, a different format allows for more detailed coverage — this is not a picture book. To make a connected narrative, I have divided the book into five sections with articles to illustrate each topic. It has been necessary to rearrange some of the material — shortening or combining some of the articles, adding to others — in other words I have edited and polished, which is part of the fun of writing. The date at the end of each article indicates when the original version appeared in *The Local*.

Why another book on Cornwall? This work differs from previous histories in one important aspect. The "Bits of History" presented here come from the columns of the town's weekly newspaper which, under different names, has been published continuously for over a hundred years. Direct quotations convey the flavor of a description, an opinion or issue as editors stamped their individual viewpoints on community events. This raw material — sometimes inaccurate and opinionated, always colorful— reveals at first hand a community coming to grips with its day-to-day problems.

Old newspapers capture our interest by their ability to edify and entertain. Seniors have their memories jogged by events long forgotten while newcomers gain a knowledge of the past. From a vantage point near the century's end, we smugly compare our standard of living with that of a hundred years ago, or less. The fashions once in vogue amuse us and we laugh at the fads and foibles of generations past. We exclaim at the ridiculously low cost of living and at the backbreaking toil of housekeeping.

Old newspapers are filled with a fascinating array of facts and figures. The date of an ancient building, the former occupants of a house, the traditions of a school or institution, the results of hotly debated elections, the historical milestones of a community — all can have a personal meaning. And we can also relate to the people — the storekeepers, clergymen, the teachers, doctors, farmers, housewives — whose lives form the fabric of a small town.

Journalist Mark Sullivan once referred to newspapers as "the diaries of history." Here are some entries from Cornwall's diary.

Janet Dempsey
May 15, 1997

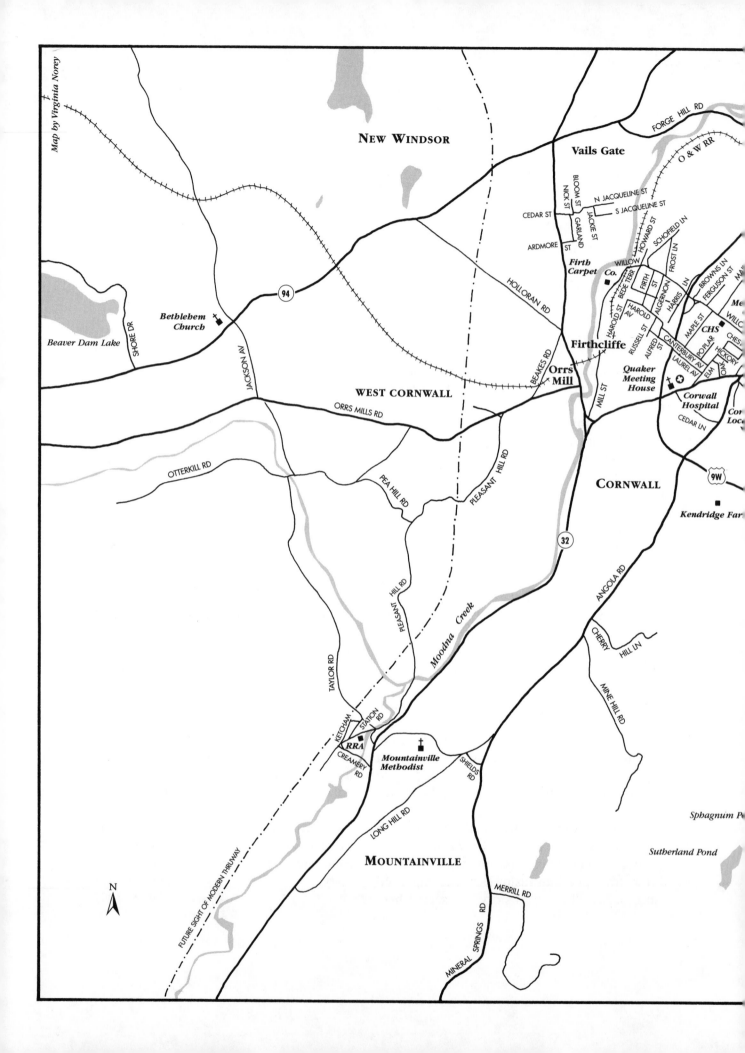

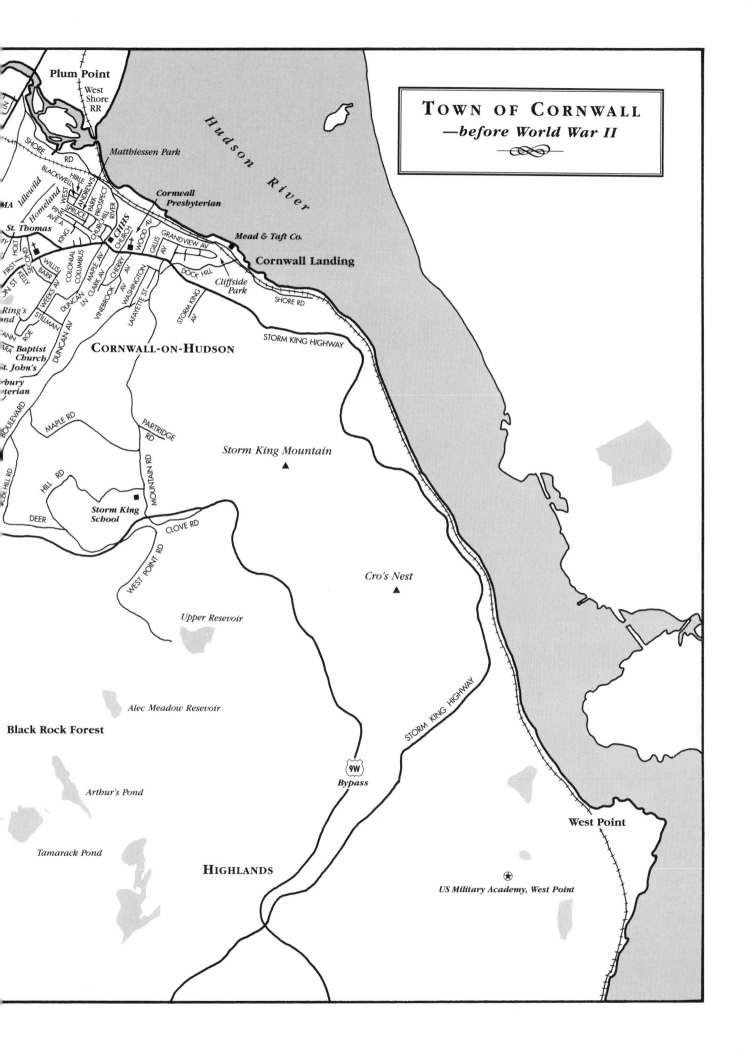

Plum Point

West Shore RR

Hudson River

Matthiessen Park

SHORE RD

BLACKWELL

HIRLE

WEST

ANDREWS

PARK

PROSPECT

RIVER

Cornwall Presbyterian

MA *Idlewild*

Homeland

PINE

SPRUCE

AVE A

CHHS

CHURCH

WOOD AV

GILLIS AV

GRANDVIEW AV

Mead & Taft Co.

Cornwall Landing

St. Thomas

KING

CHURCHILL

MAPLE AV

CHERRY AV

WASHINGTON

DOCK HILL

Cliffside Park

FIRST

HOLT

SECOND

WILLIS

BARR

COLONIAL

COLUMBUS

CLARK AV

LN

DUNCAN

VINEBROOK AV

LAFAYETTE ST

STORM KING AV

SHORE RD

Ring's nd

ANN

ARA

WEEKS AV

ROE

STILLMAN

DUNCAN AV

CORNWALL-ON-HUDSON

STORM KING HIGHWAY

Baptist Church

t. John's

rbury terian

BOULEVARD

MAPLE RD

PARTRIDGE RD

Storm King Mountain

▲

CK HILL RD

HILL RD

MOUNTAIN RD

DEER

Storm King School

◼

CLOVE RD

WEST POINT RD

Cro's Nest

▲

Upper Resevoir

Alec Meadow Resevoir

Black Rock Forest

Arthur's Pond

STORM KING HIGHWAY

🛡9W🛡

Bypass

West Point

Tamarack Pond

HIGHLANDS

✪

US Military Academy, West Point

THE CORNWALL NEWPAPERS

Since the Cornwall newspapers form the basis for the articles in this volume, it is pertinent to examine their style and substance. *The Local* was not the first weekly to appear in Cornwall; it was preceded in 1870 by a small sheet called *The Cornwall Paper,* published by Peter P. Hazen, storekeeper, and Nicholas Chatfield, Sr., a tanner. Surviving for less than a year, this paper was followed by a more permanent venture lasting about ten years — *The Cornwall Times*, its editor Miss Sarah J.A. Hussey, a woman of education and refinement. Her paper's blend of culture, temperance literature and "society" news was a strong contrast to the homespun production of Hazen and Chatfield and to the strident rival weekly which appeared soon afterward. Named *The Cornwall Reflector*, its aim was "To Reflect the Best Interests of Cornwall." It was published by Henry H. Snelling, a cabinetmaker by trade. In his struggles to keep the newspaper going, Snelling received encouragement and financial assistance from Lawson Valentine[1] of Houghton Farm in Mountainville. Snelling later became blind and in 1892 left Cornwall for an institution in St. Louis where he died in December, 1897.

It is unfortunate that the newspaper files of 1888 and 1889 are missing, but an item from May 5, 1933 states: "45 years ago this issue — *The Cornwall Local* succeeded *The Cornwall Reflector* under the management of H.A. Gates publisher and E.P. Thompson, assistant editor." Presumably the new newspaper took over the facilities of *The Reflector*. We can turn to the town business directories for further elucidation. The final entry for *The Reflector* is in 1887; H. A. Gates is listed as editor and proprietor of *The Cornwall Local* in 1888 and 1889, Thomas Pendell in 1890 and 1891, Cady and Goodnough in 1892.

When *The Local* was advertised for sale in 1892, the owner was given as C.P. Brate, the editor, Pendell. The newspaper was bought by a young couple from Pennsylvania, L. Grant Goodnough and his wife Belle, in partnership with an uncle, Abijah Cady (who soon returned to his more lucrative trade of mason). Under the Goodnoughs, *The Local* prospered. A determination to succeed in the face of many obstacles challenged the couple to produce an up-to-date newspaper attuned to the community it represented. Discarding the fillers of their predecessors — the moral tracts and serialized stories — the Goodnoughs concentrated on issues of genuine interest to their readers: local elections; community improvements such as roads, sidewalks and a new water supply system; church and organization news and the inevitable record of births, marriages and deaths which marks the passage from one generation to the next. Will Cornwall support a new school? How does the town stand on the issue of liquor licenses? Who will be the next village mayor, the next town supervisor? How does Cornwall react to the first automobile on its streets and the first airplane to land in the town? What about giving women the vote? These are some of the topics covered by the new editor.

The Goodnoughs retired in 1919, selling the newspaper to Dr. Ernest G. Stillman who hired Creswell Maclaughlin as editor. During the latter's two-year tenure, the paper took on a different tone — crusading, lively and satirical. Then came a series of less competent editors, under whose direction some of the

---

1   Valentine (1828-1891) was a manufacturer of paints and varnishes. He was connected through marriage with Houghton-Mifflin Publishing Company.

zest was lost. When Raymond S. Preston became the owner and editor in 1930, he moved the office from the corner of Willow Avenue to a small building on his Hasbrouck Avenue property—where it has been located ever since.

As each new editor changed the paper's focus, they gave it a different format and a new name—from *The Cornwall Local* to *The Local-Press* in 1908, to *Cornwall Press* in 1914 and *The Cornwall Press* in 1922; and back to *The Cornwall Local* in 1923. I have often referred to the newspaper simply as *The Local*.

August 4, 1892

In 1892 *The Cornwall Local* was only four years old, a slim four-page weekly published by L.C. Goodnough and A. Cady; it sold for five cents a copy, one dollar per year. The general format bore no resemblance to today's newspaper. The front page contained brief items on national and world news, mostly sensational in nature. Fillers took up the back page: articles from periodicals, excerpts from sermons, serialized stories. It was on the two inside pages that the local news was to be found — short items jumbled together at random: personals, obits, business matters, letters. The many ads occupied the outside columns of all four pages.

Selecting August 4, 1892, let us see what can be learned about life in the Nineties. The general news on page one includes three strikes, the confessions of a murderer, "Anarchists Talk in Newark," the launching of a cruiser, the Brooklyn. A story headlined "Her Mother Said Nay" tells about a Philadelphia socialite who elopes with a postal clerk, to the mortification of her family. Another column lists the current market prices of such commodities as foodstuffs, grain and furs. One article describes a nationwide hot spell: "The average temperature for the eight days during which the heat wave prevailed was 91 degrees, exceeding all previous record." One hundred sixteen deaths were attributed to the heat and countless cases of heat prostration. A joke column is another front-page feature, a sample: "Penelope - Why do you say Charley Nixen is like a spyglass? Answer - Because I can draw him out, see right through him, and when I am tired of him, shut him up."

On the back page one can peruse such articles as "Accidents and Incidents in Everyday Life," "Popular Science Notes," an account of a national Y.P.S.C.E. conference at Madison Square Garden (the Young People's Society of Christian Endeavor); and there is a lengthy ad for Dr. William's Pink Pills entitled "A Detroit Miracle." We must turn to the inside pages for the local news. Cornwall, too, has suffered from the heat. Some stores and other business places have closed early, and John Tompkins of Mountainville, a venerable Civil War veteran, was overcome by the heat while working in a hayfield. Despite the weather, Cornwall is "a paradise for babies" as "not a single child has died in almost a year." Crime is present in the form of a chicken thief who visits Roe Town (Mailler Avenue) one night and makes off with twenty-five of Mrs. Crissey's chickens.

Cornwallites can look forward to two fairs—one at the Episcopal Church, the other at the school on Clinton Street put on by the Canterbury Fire Company, at which the Cornwall Band "will render fine music on the grounds." "The ladies have nobly assisted the firemen in the preparation and have neglected no effort to render the coming fair and festival well worth a visit from everyone."

Three hundred passengers disembarked from the *Mary Powell* the previous weekend bound for Cornwall hotels and boarding places. "A progressive euchre party took place at the Elmer .... There were five tables and the game lasted two hours." The first prize for ladies was an Indian kettle, for the men, a pipe. Commented *The Local* "...the Elmer is one of the most delightful of summer houses." Silverman's apartment house on Hudson Street later occupied a portion of the former hotel. Another recent event was a concert by the Dudley Buck Quartette, described as "all that could be desired" and making a profit of over one hundred dollars.

News from the waterfront: a shipment of

several thousand feet of lumber by building contractor Holland Emslie; Leonard P. Clark, an expert boat builder, sends a canoe he has made to Galveston, Texas. "Reuben Clark has a very intelligent dog, popularly known as Shep, who on the approach of a boat will grab the rope and ring the bell and run into the office of Mr. Clark." And the West Shore Railroad uses one hundred gallons of water each day from the spring on Dock Hill.

The Mountainville correspondent, Columbine, writes that "Mr. B. Wright has some of the finest looking corn in this vicinity" and there is an abundance of huckleberries on Schunnemunck Mountain. She deplores much "drunkenness" in her part of town. "Thomas Taft, G.S. Talbot, George Stevenson and others attended the prohibition convention in Newburgh yesterday. They report a good attendance and any amount of enthusiasm and determination." Cornwall will soon vote to become a dry town.

The Cromwell Guards, a social and athletic club, meets regularly; among its activities are shooting matches at the present Donahue Farm. For the more serious, Rev. George Egbert of the Canterbury Presbyterian Church is holding weekly classes in English and Parliamentary Law.

One letter stresses the need for a road linking the Boulevard with Hudson Street. A suggested route across the Cocks and Roe properties closely parallels the present Payson Road. A pathetic item refers to H. H. Snelling, editor of *The Cornwall Reflector*, who has lost his eyesight. Travel expenses to St. Louis, where he will enter a home, also clothing and money for his support, have been contributed by local churches and townspeople.

An account of the annual school meeting of District No. 4 (Cornwall-on-Hudson) lists total school taxes as $4,397.19 and state aid of $1,224.09. Teachers' wages cost the district $3,892.40, janitorial service $310.00, books and stationery $153.16, fuel $127.50, repairs and supplies $134.25. The school was then located in the rear portion of the brick apartment house on Idlewild Avenue. The larger front section came in 1896 when high school status had been achieved. Elected to the school board were Carlos H. Stone, headmaster of Stone School (now Storm King School), George H. Horobin, a long-time Mead and Taft Company employee and clerk of the board, Henry L. Barton, and Martha C. Cocks (women could serve on school boards).

The issue contains a sly gibe at Cornwall's neighbor to the south: "Highland Falls is reported as having 138 old maids to deal with."

July 29, 1992

L. Grant Goodnough, Editor

The Goodnoughs had taken over *The Local* in June 1892. By June of 1896, the editor could report: "Four years ago today we first arrived in our beautiful village, and they have been four years of constant thought and study on our part to improve our paper. Have we succeeded? We say yes, with a capital Y. Four years ago we commenced with two apprentices, and hardly enough for them to do." Besides Goodnough and his wife (who did much of the writing), seven people were now employed, and the number of subscribers had tripled. The newspaper had moved into larger quarters next to the Storm King Engine House, where there was room for a modern press and other needed equipment. "We shall make catalogue work a specialty," Goodnough had declared, and soon the office was receiving orders to print their annual catalogues from Dwyer's Nursery, the Baker-Rose Sanitarium and the Orrs Mills Poultry Yard.

In 1900 the office moved again, to the building adjoining the Cornwall Presbyterian Church, which was doubled in size to make room for all sorts of new equipment. Goodnough installed two electric motors to replace the water power which had previously run the presses. There were other innovations: an 8-page format instead of the smaller 4-page paper; a change in name to *The Local Press*, then to the *Cornwall Press* and an increase in price from one dollar to $1.50 per year. At the time of the disastrous flood of 1903, the great demand for the newspaper exceeded the supply on hand.

3

Goodnough's twenty-seven years as editor (1892-1919) spanned a period of much change. By the 1890s, Cornwall's prominence as a summer resort was ending; its economy would now depend more on such industries as the Firth Carpet and Mead and Taft Companies. *The Local* recorded this transformation; also the coming of electric lights, telephones, a water supply system, as well as a steady growth in population. Formerly "Independent with Democratic leanings," *The Local* became a Republican newspaper in line with the editor's own affiliation as well as most of the town's. The chief political controversies, however, were not between Republicans and Democrats, but were those generated by heated local elections.

When the aqueduct for New York City's water supply was being constructed through the town, *The Local* reported on the mammoth project—from the planning stage to the opening ceremonies a decade later. The problems connected with the great engineering feat of building the Storm King Highway was front-page news for many years. When the outbreak of World War I brought troops here to guard the aqueduct, and later called up Cornwall men and women to serve their country. *The Local* covered these wartime events. It printed biographical sketches of the servicemen and their pictures, letters from the front, and reports on civilian war relief efforts.

Each year on the anniversary of his purchase of *The Local*, Goodnough would use the occasion for self-congratulation, boasting of the increase in jobs, advertising and circulation; describing the installation of up-to-date machines which made the newspaper office "second in working equipment to none in the country," and reporting on the paper's sound financial condition. The summary would close with an expression of the editor's appreciation for the public's patronage and support.

At the time of the sale of *The Local* in 1919, the Goodnoughs received a letter from Rev. Lyman Abbott,[2] one of Cornwall's foremost citizens. "My dear Mr. Goodnough," he wrote, "We are all sorry to see the announcement of your sale of *The Cornwall Press* in this week's issue. It is not too much to say that you and Mrs. Goodnough have really created it, and in doing so have made an excellent local paper — I have never known a better .... Under your united management, *The Press* has always stood for the best interest of Cornwall... In common with all your fellow citizens the Abbotts will be very glad to hear that you are to continue to make Cornwall your hometown."

The Goodnoughs did stay in Cornwall, spending their last years in a charming old house on Avenue A. He died in 1933, Mrs. Goodnough in 1938. Two years before, she had written a series of reminiscences of their twenty-seven years at *The Local*, a valuable source of Cornwall history.

March 17, 1993

Creswell Maclaughlin, Editor

"No country newspaper man can clothe himself in the gorgeous panoply of seven suits and two over coats and hope to achieve financial success." This taunt from L. Grant Goodnough, editor of *The Cornwall Local*, was directed at Creswell Maclaughlin, one of Cornwall's most controversial figures —a fellow journalist, writer, orator, bon vivant; a thorn in the flesh of many a respectable citizen, for no one was safe from his sarcastic wit.

In the summer of 1895, Maclaughlin, then in his early thirties, came to the Gold Cure Sanitarium[3] in Cornwall to take a treatment for alcoholism. His debut in *The Local* was a

---

2   Lyman Abbott (1835-1922) was a well-known clergyman, author and editor of *The Outlook*. He made his home in Cornwall for over sixty years.

3   The Baker-Rose Gold Cure Sanitarium opened in the 1890s for the treatment of alcohol and drug addiction by a method called the "Gold Cure."

column entitled "A Jerseyman's Notes" in which he described life at the facility. "The boys at the Sanitarium have as good a time as at any of the hotels .... The variety of life represented by the different patients makes up an interesting company when they get together on the broad porch in the evening. Some of the men are excellent musicians, others are brilliant wits. A little leading brings them out and time passes gaily...A kind of fellowship reigns over all and harmony holds her own." Two years later Maclaughlin married Miss Leila Jaeger, "one of Cornwall's most charming young ladies."

Already his reputation as a maverick had been recognized. Wrote *The Local* editor. "Probably no one who ever came to Cornwall became so well known in so short a time as Mr. Maclaughlin. He possesses a style of writing peculiarly his own, and in his inimitable way, ridicules the fads, follies and pleasures of any community in which his lot may be cast." In future years, editor Goodnough would be less charitable.

Maclaughlin was a native of Jersey City. He left school at sixteen for a job as assistant librarian at an engineering society. Next he embarked on a career of journalism, working on *The Jersey City Democrat*, several Boston newspapers as well as *The New York Sun* and *New York World*. Whether this frequent change of jobs can be attributed to his outspoken opinions or to bouts with alcoholism is not known. After moving to Cornwall, he became editor of *The Courier*, a short-lived weekly of the early 1900s, and published a small magazine, *The Schoolmaster*, for a few years. While editing these publications, Maclaughlin was also sought after for speaking engagements — he is remembered as an eloquent and witty speaker.

None of these activities was especially lucrative, and in 1904 Maclaughlin filed for bankruptcy, listing debts of seven thousand dollars and assets of less than one thousand including stock of dubious value in *The Courier* and *The Schoolmaster*. Among his many creditors were Governor Odell and other well-known figures, also New York City tailors, restaurants and hotels. *The Local* was not averse to giving full coverage to the misfortune, quoting from several city newspapers, and quick to correct the notion that Maclaughlin was connected with *The Local*. "Mr. Maclaughlin is a bright, ready writer and speaker," commented Goodnough, "and a pleasant gentleman to meet (when he feels good-natured) but unfortunately he possesses too expensive inclinations for a country newspaper man" (he must have been thinking of the seven suits and two overcoats), and he condemned "a seemingly evident intent to defraud the public, or at least anyone whom he could persuade to lend him money..."

The feud between the two editors erupted in full-fledged fury at the time of the Hudson-Fulton Celebration of 1909—this episode will be described elsewhere. With more important topics demanding public attention, there is no mention of Maclaughlin throughout the war years. In 1919, when Goodnough retired and sold the Cornwall paper to Dr. Ernest G. Stillman as part of the Cornwall Industrial Corporation consortium, he must have been dismayed to find Maclaughlin replacing him as editor.

Under the new management, the *Cornwall-Press* (as it was then called) was a very different newspaper. Maclaughlin's own views, often expressed in a witty or satirical manner, were not confined to the editorials but spilled over into a column entitled "The Grill Room" and were sometimes appended to the news items. Far from the temperance position traditionally taken by the paper, the new editor treated prohibition as a huge joke, not to be taken seriously. In reporting one arrest for violation of the Volstead Act,[4] he placed emphasis on the fact that the building where the sale of liquor took place was owned by a prominent citizen.

Maclaughlin gave the "upper classes" scant coverage and was not careful about the spelling of names and other details. Church news, formerly an important part of the paper, was drastically reduced by a charge of advertising rates for church items. In defense of the new policy, Maclaughlin pointed out that since he had become editor, the *Cornwall-Press* had done more for the welfare of Corn-

4   Passed by Congress in 1919 to enforce the 18th Amendment prohibiting the sale of intoxicating liquor.

wall than all of the churches combined! One of his goals was an exposé of entrenched authority; his serious, well-written editorials on the necessity of working for community betterment show Maclaughlin at his best. His job as editor lasted until 1922.

During the next quarter century, Maclaughlin's name appeared only occasionally in the newspaper he had once edited, although he continued to live in Cornwall. He had a job for a time at *The Newburgh News* where his son also worked, and his skill as orator made him a sought-after speaker. He died in 1946 after a second leg amputation. The obituary lauds him as "one of Cornwall's best known personages," a frequent contributor to magazines and periodicals and, according to *The Saturday Evening Post*, one of the six best after dinner speakers of his day. His address on George Washington was considered the finest of the speeches presented during the 1932 Bicentennial of Washington's birth.

Such was Creswell Maclaughlin — a unique figure in the annals of Cornwall history.

March 10, 1993

PLACES

This section identifies some of the streets in Cornwall, then takes the reader on a tour of the most populous parts of the town. A history of two major industries follows and a look at several of the buildings which were then prominent, such as a busy store, a crude gymnasium, and Cornwall's most historic home.

For newcomers to the community or strangers, it should be explained that Cornwall refers to *two* entities: the town and the incorporated village bordering the Hudson River which lies within the town limits (and is now known as Cornwall-on-Hudson to correspond with the post office). Main Street traverses a part of the town called Canterbury by old timers or the "upper village" to differentiate it from the "lower village" or Cornwall-on-Hudson. Willow Avenue leads to Firthcliffe, west of Route 9W; Mountainville is a rural community south of Canterbury. "The Mountain" is a section of the town along Deer Hill, Maple and Mountain Roads. Cornwall Landing, now gone, was once an active business, transportation and residential center along the riverfront.

Other places mentioned are the schools: the New York Military Academy — N.Y.M.A.; C.H.S. for the Cornwall High School on Willow Avenue; and C.H.H.S. for the Cornwall-on-Hudson High School on Hudson Street.

Streets and Roads

It has been said that street names record the history of a town; this statement is borne out by many of the older Cornwall roads.

The local street names fall into several categories. Some have a botanical derivation such as the tree streets: Spruce, Pine and Cherry in Cornwall-on-Hudson; and Willow Avenue, Oak, Elm, Chestnut, Walnut and Cedar in Cornwall. There are three Maples — one in each village and another on the mountain; also Laurel and Vinebrook Avenues. Two roads are named for an animal being seen in increasing numbers: Deer Hill and Fawn Hill Roads.

Streets with topographical names include Long Hill, Meadow and Pleasant Hill; also Ridge, Mineral Spring and Mountain Roads. Some streets celebrate the Hudson Valley: Bay View, Grand View, River and Storm King Avenues, Hudson Street and Shore Road.

Most streets, however, derive their names from local places and people. Academy Avenue borders N.Y.M.A. Orr's Mills Road starts near the site of a mill once operated by the Orr family; nearby Station Road once led to a station on the Erie Railroad. Homeland Avenue traverses a former estate of that name. Idlewild Park Drive follows the road which led to the home of the writer Nathaniel P. Willis, who called his estate "Idlewild"; there is also an Idlewild Avenue. Two streets have a religious connotation: Quaker Avenue for the old Quaker Meeting House and Church Street which runs alongside the Cornwall Presbyterian Church.

Taft Place memorializes a prominent family whose firm, Mead and Taft, erected many fine buildings, both in Cornwall and other communities. Another important industry was the Firth Carpet Company, which gave its name to Firthcliffe, and to Mill, Firth and Algernon Streets.

Taylor Place—with its patriotic streets, Washington and Lafayette, is named for Harvey R. Taylor, a building contractor who developed the site. Nearby is Payson Road which borrows the middle name of the writer, Edward Payson Roe, and crosses his land. The Weeks Estate gets its name from Thomas W. Weeks who lived in the columned mansion on Duncan Avenue and owned much adjacent land. Here are Weeks and Stillman Avenues (the latter joins Duncan Avenue near The Grail, a former Stillman home), and three author streets: Roe, Willis and Barr (for Amelia E. Barr who had a summer home on the mountain).

Cornwall-on-Hudson has other streets named for early residents. There is Clark Avenue for the original owners of much of the village; Duncan Avenue for Colonel James Duncan, a Mexican War hero; Churchill Street for an early developer of that section, the same for Wood Avenue. Curie Road is named for the Charles Curie family, owners of "Idlewild" at the turn of the century; Wilson Road (formerly Gillis Lane)—both families occupied the old brick house at the end of the street.

The upper village (or Canterbury, as it was formerly called) has a Clinton Street for Dr. Alexander Clinton who once lived there, and Hasbrouck Avenue for William C. Hasbrouck whose property extended to the Boulevard and beyond. Several Firthcliffe streets are named for old residents of that section of town:

Schofield, Howard and Frost. Mailler Avenue recalls the family of that name whose house stands at the intersection of Willow and Mailler Avenues.

Mountainville has Ketcham Avenue for the first settlers in that area and Taylor Road for a family whose farms extended along its route. Beakes Road comes from a large land-owner who had a race track on his property.

In conclusion, the most uninspired street names: Avenues A and B and First and Second Streets—and the most unusual—Angola Road. Mrs. Robert Hume, town historian in the 1950s, grew up on the latter road and did research on the derivation of the name. According to her findings, "Descendants of early families ... speak of hearing a legend of an old negro who lived somewhere between the junction of Angola and Mineral Spring Roads .... The surmise: ... there may have been an early family ... in this section of which this man was the only survivor." Her theory was strengthened by a reference in *The Narratives of New Netherlands* to a number of slaves having been imported to the Hudson Valley from Angola in Africa.

These are some Cornwall roads for joggers and weekend strollers to explore; the exact locations have been omitted to add a challenge to your excursions.

April 24, 1991

A Tour of Cornwall, I

The Cornwall history by Lewis Beach, written in the 1870s, has a chapter entitled "Walks and Drives" in which the author takes his readers on a tour of the town, pointing out interesting sights along the main thoroughfares. The next two articles will employ the same strategy. As the days grow longer and warmer and the temptation to be outdoors increases, these "Bits of History" may be an inducement to explore the town on foot.

The riverfront is a good place to start. The spacious and scenic park at the river's edge is

comparatively new; it used to be the site of Mead and Taft Company, a building and contracting firm whose large brick structure faced the depot of the West Shore Railroad. Near the present boat-launching ramp was a dock where the graceful river steamers landed. The Yacht Club occupies the site of other docks and of the Stillman boathouse. A relic of the 19th century is a tiny building, seemingly a storage shed, but once a Quaker meeting place. After crossing the railroad tracks, Shore Road continued on as far as Deane's

Point where a family of that name had a summer residence. There were other houses nearby and a precipitous winding road, Jacob's Ladder, which led up the hill to Bay View Avenue. This area was drastically altered some years ago by preliminary activities for the Con Ed project.[1]

Dock Hill, across from the park, leads up to the village. A foundation wall of the Cornwall Landing post office can be seen on the right, and on the opposite side is evidence of the houses which once perched precariously above the brook. Bay View Avenue, branching off at the top of the hill, was formerly dotted with summer boarding houses, many of them owned by members of the Clark family. The Donahue Farm, long the scene of Cornwall's Independence Day Celebration, was known as Cold Spring Farm (for the spring on Dock Hill) when owned by Albrecht Pagenstecher early in the present century. It was originally part of the Clark holdings which extended far up into the mountains. Farther along, the large house on the left (once Clark's) used to be a restaurant, the Storm King Arms. It opened in the early 1920s, about the same time as The Half Moon Inn, a small house tucked into the hillside at the entrance to the Storm King Highway. Along an old road paralleling this route were summer boarding establishments: the Eureka, a stately mansion once a private home, and the Birdsall House—the foundation holes of both are easy to spot.

The other end of Bay View Avenue joins Hudson Street. The former Silverman apartment house is on the site of the 18th-century home of Reuben Clark; after being greatly enlarged, it became the Elmer House, an exclusive summer hotel. The antique shop at the corner of Cherry Avenue and Hudson Street was Cocks' Store, where generations of townspeople shopped for groceries. In the building next to the Presbyterian Church *The Cornwall Local* was published for a number of years. The elementary school stands on the site of the Smith House Cottage (scarcely a cottage by modern definition) which was relocated on River Avenue behind the bandstand. Between the short street near the school and River Avenue, now a parking lot, stood the Smith House—part brick, part wood, three stories high—one of the first of Cornwall's resort hotels. When its days of grandeur were over, the building deteriorated rapidly to shabby apartments and commercial uses—even a garage. The present post office, across the street, was once a livery stable, later a garage.

The building now occupied by a bar and auction gallery was built in the 1930s to house the Storm King Theatre. It replaced an older structure, Matthiessen Hall, an impressive brick building which lent dignity to the Village Square. The first floor contained, at various periods, a bank, post office, stores and a tearoom. Upstairs were the public library and business offices. The third floor auditorium was used for school functions, athletic events, movies, lectures, fairs and dances.

Nearby on Idlewild Avenue stood the high school, now an apartment house. Across the street, on the library lot, was the final location of the original bandstand when forced by automobile traffic to be moved from the center of the Square. On the Spruce Street end of the block was the gymnasium of the Garden Athletic Club which later became the headquarters of the American Legion.

Back at the Square, the vacant property across from the old theater used to contain the Weeks building, which had stores on the ground floor and an assembly room above where several fraternal lodges met. Later it became known as Santoro's for the restaurant and bar run by the Santoro family. On the site of the modern bandstand was a meat market owned by Ulysses Grant Clark, one of several Clark butchers. This small building had been moved from the Duncan Avenue corner to make room for the Telephone Building, later the dental offices of Dr. David L. Dorfman, now of Dr. Michael Seitz.

Proceeding up Hudson Street one passes three former boarding houses. The Cornwall Inn, once the Elm Park, was a year-round hotel, with a long succession of proprietors.

---

1   The pumped storage hydroelectric plant which Consolidated Edison proposed to build at Storm King Mounrtain. After a 17 year legal battle (1963-1980), the project was abandoned.

9

In the next block is an apartment building, once the school of Alfred C. Roe, then the Palmer House, a summer resort, and in later years, the Gold Cure Sanitarium. Across the street was the Wiley House which opened in the summer for boarders.

April 1, 1992

A Tour of Cornwall, II

To continue our tour of Cornwall, many Cornwallites remember the former Catholic Church which served its congregants for almost a century. All that remains of the original group of buildings is the parochial school, now replaced by a much larger facility. Old timers called the adjacent section around First and Second Streets the Fourth Ward (possibly an election designation). When the aqueduct was under construction, the long, low house on the west side of Hudson Street was the headquarters of the aqueduct police. The village limits are at the traffic sign across from the food store—the corporation line, it used to be called. This area near the Town Park was built up at an early date, a collection of small houses, clustered closely together. It had the name of Garnerville, probably a corruption of Gardiner, the name of a black family who owned land there. The wooded knoll, then more extensive, was a popular picnic grove.

River Light Park was for years the grounds of the Emma L. Hardy Memorial Home for the Blind,[2] usually shortened to the Blind Home. Each summer groups of adults and children from New York City came here for a two-week vacation, and many town organizations and church groups dispensed hospitality in the form of outings and entertainment. The main house on the property (razed in 1985) had been the home of Clementine Talmadge, a Sands-Ring descendant. Her brother Charles Ring lived in an adjoining house on the site of the Little League playing fields. It was one of Cornwall's best known summer boarding houses, the Linden Park House. Rings' Pond was a favorite fishing spot, and in the winter, skating races were held there.

On the Town Hall parking lot, there used to be two frame houses, the sanitarium of Dr. Henry Lyle Winter. Later, Col. H.G. Stanton acquired the property for his school, which prepared students for the U.S. service academies; he added the present Town Hall building for classrooms and a dormitory.

Many of the structures on Main Street date from before the turn of the century— only a few will be mentioned here. On the east side of the street is the large white house of Leon Garvin—once a private school. Farther along is the Lemon-Callahan building, the former Cornwall National Bank; then the old firehouse; and Hey's, for many years the Union Hotel. To create the parking lot, an old house was destroyed which had been a 19th-century post office and lawyer's office. The large brick building on the west side of the street was Harry Keevill's Cornwall Garage; at the corner of Willow Avenue was the Masonic Temple, erected after World War I for the Cornwall Industrial Corporation. Smitchger's was once a post office; Bridge Street separated Clark's Meat Market from Hazard's (formerly Holloran's) Pharmacy.

Several "Bits of History" can be found along Willow Avenue. Behind the Masonic Temple is a very old building, the Atkinson Woolen Mill, powered by water from the creek. The next owner was Harvey R. Taylor, a prosperous contractor and builder; then came Mahlon Wood. The apartment complex on the north side of Willow Avenue covers the

---

2 This facility, operated by the New York Association for the Blind, was established in 1911 to provide a vacation home for the blind.

summer estate of Herman Trost, later of Sol Levy. The brick house across the street was probably built by a member of the Fancher family. Next door is "Sunset Cottage," the former home of the Emslies.

The Willow Avenue School, originally the Cornwall High School, was built early in the present century; its size doubled in 1930s with an addition on the west end. Forty years later, the original building was replaced by a new wing. The two large houses across the street were part of the Brewster farm, which once extended from Mailler Avenue to Main Street near the high school.

At the corner of Mailler Avenue is the Hunter-Mailler house; a Hunter daughter married Floyd Mailler and the family lived there for a long time. Near Route 9W, a large house on the south side was once a boarding house, a private school, and the home of Dr. Palmer Bowdish. The Abell house, now boarded up, was the home of Henry E. Abell, a retired police comissioner.[3] In olden times, Mr. Abell permitted organizations to picnic in his woods, and on July Fourth, he would invite the neighbors to a fireworks display.

On the same side of Willow Avenue could be seen the Firthcliffe bandstand, the firehouse, and the Firthcliffe Club. This building had been erected by the Firth Carpet Company for its employees. For many years, Bob Smith's barber shop occupied one of the front rooms. In 1970, the clubhouse, then owned by Sal Macri, burned to the ground. Near the foot of the hill, there used to be a dangerous underpass which had to be negotiated to reach the mill. This tunnel lay beneath the tracks of the Ontario and Western Railroad; the station stood on the hill nearby.

The conglomeration of dilapidated structures along Moodna Creek used to house the Firth Carpet Company, a large and prosperous firm. Firth had come to Cornwall in 1886; gradually, over the years, the company expanded, erecting larger buildings and installing modern equipment. Along Mill Street remain some of the houses built for the workers. When Firth, later called Mohasco, closed the Cornwall plant in the mid 1960s, Majestic Weaving Company took over the facility until it went bankrupt in 1981.

April 8, 1992

The Garden Athletic Club Gymnasium

On the afternoon of Saturday, January 21, 1914, the townspeople of Cornwall gathered in a plain one-story building to witness the laying of its cornerstone. Following Rev. Lyman Abbott's dedicatory prayer and selections by the Village Band, the keys of the building were presented to the chairwoman and the cornerstone placed, after which everyone had refreshments. There was nothing pretentious about the place in which these ceremonies were taking place. It was a small frame structure, stained brown, with white trim and a tarpaper roof, its rudimentary heating system and electricity the only amenities. What made the occasion so special was that the building was a gymnasium which had been

built, not by federal grants or taxes, but under the sponsorship of a Cornwall organization known as the Garden Athletic Club.

Our story begins in 1909; at least that is when the club is first mentioned in an editorial: "It is a fact that the village is notably devoid of opportunities for the occupation of mind and body of the children outside of school hours and the garden club is formed to meet this deficiency. It gives to the boys an interesting and profitable manner of spending their leisure hours." And that June there was a "Grand Musicale" at the Cornwall Presbyterian Church "to raise funds for the furtherance and advancement of the boys' labors."

The Garden Athletic Club had been

---

3 The house has been razed and replaced by a modern professional building.

started by Miss Beatrice V. Abbott, daughter of Lyman Abbott, Cornwall's distinguished clergyman, writer and sage. After her mother's death in 1907, Miss Abbott undoubtedly spent more time at home with her father; the idea of the club may have come from him. At any rate, a portion of the Abbott grounds on Clark Avenue was divided into small plots; here the boys planted vegetables which they tended and harvested to sell to the villagers; the profits went for athletic activities.

In the course of the next few years, several club events made the newspaper: the games they played, fund-raisers, and the formation of a girls' group. Their big undertaking came about because of renovations being made to Matthiessen Hall, the large building in the Village Square. It was decided to ban sports events from its newly decorated auditorium—which left the village with no gym. The next development was when, in the fall of 1914, the Board of Education granted Miss Abbott permission to erect a building on school grounds "for the benefit of the Garden Clubs, Camp Fire Girls and Boy Scouts." The Board would assume no responsibility except for a voice in the management; and if no longer occupied by the clubs, the building would revert to the school district.

Miss Abbott and her committee wasted no time; they negotiated a loan and hired the building firm of Jaeger Brothers. Reported the *Cornwall Press* of November 20th: "The New Building is Staked Out - the simplest and smallest that will answer the purpose .... The new enterprise ... deserves the unstinted cooperation of Cornwall-on-Hudson people." The next week there was more: "The Boys of the Garden Club have commenced excavating for the new gymnasium building and will complete this part of the work entirely themselves. They will also assist, under Mr. Jaeger's supervision, in the construction of the building itself." Two months later the gym was finished. It stood across from the school on Idlewild Avenue, at the rear of the lot now occupied by the library. It was a small building, 38x52 feet, containing a basketball court and two dressing rooms.

Almost at once the gym was fully rented. The executive committee headed by Miss Abbott, formulated a few rules: a closing hour of midnight, no dances without a chaperone approved by the committee, no basketball practice without an approved coach. The rent schedule was as follows: 20¢ or 40¢ an hour for practice sessions, depending on the use of electric lights, five dollars for evening entertainments, two-fifty for daytime events. The janitorial service was undertaken by the Garden Club boys themselves— Leo Fanning, the first janitor, was a stickler about muddy boots!

"It is very evident that a long-felt want has been supplied," commented the newspaper. In fact, the gym was so popular that practice teams had to leave promptly to make way for the next group. Besides team practice, the Garden Clubs met there, also the Camp Fire Girls and the Y.M.C.A. Several evenings a week were reserved for gym classes, one of them supervised by George Toombs, the village policeman. The rental income supplemented by benefits paid the current expenses and interest on the debt, even some of the principal. Plays put on by Stone School and a local dramatic club, a series of "victrola dances" and a fair by the Girls' Club were some of the fund-raisers. Lavatories were soon added and a brick walk leading from Idlewild Avenue.

In 1915 the Garden Athletic Club team had a busy schedule, playing Haverstraw and Kingston as well as home teams: the Firthcliffe Orioles, C.H.H.S. and Stone School. The basketball season of 1916 opened with the G.A.C. team—Leo Fanning, captain, and James O'Mara, Russell Talbot, George Ellingham, Robert and Harold Britnell—defeating Cornwall High School 31-12. After the game there was dancing with music by Collins and Carey of Newburgh. Meanwhile, the boys continued to work on their gardens; the money from the produce they sold went to the gymnasium fund. One year they sent a garden exhibit to the State Fair at Syracuse.

America's entry in World War I lessened the ranks of the G.A.C., and after the new high school on Hudson Street opened in 1924, the gym was no longer needed. It next became the headquarters of the American Legion until the 1930s, when it was considered an eyesore and torn down after the building of the new library.

Today nothing remains of the G.A.C. gym

but a foundation hole; nevertheless, it symbolizes the sterling qualities of determination, cooperation and hard work.

February 12, 1992

The Old Homestead

Last week's article told how a Cornwall youth organization, the Garden Athletic Club, built a gymnasium for sports events and other community activities. This week's topic is the Village Improvement Society, founded in 1899 by a group of civic-minded women who were dedicated to such modern causes as the environment and historic preservation. The first president was Mrs. Lyman Abbott, mother of Beatrice Abbott, who organized the Garden Athletic Club.

The society began in a small way; they deposited trash receptacles around the village and removed signs from telegraph poles and fences; they planted trees along the main streets and at the Cold Spring on Dock Hill, where they also placed a rustic bench. They landscaped a plot at the Cornwall Landing railroad station to improve the appearance of this entrance to the town, and erected drinking fountains—in the Village Square and at the new playground.

Annual contests were a popular vehicle for the society's goals. Schoolchildren received 10¢ per hundred for collecting tent caterpillar eggs, with a prize for the youngster who brought in the most. Another prize, this for the best asters, was awarded at a flower show in the fall; prizes were also given for the boys' gardens on the former E. P. Roe property (Payson Road), this project a forerunner of the Garden Athletic Club. Adults could compete in an annual contest for the most attractive dooryard, the first prize a silver cup. A number of fund-raisers—rummage sales, concerts, lectures on natural history and environmental topics—furnished income for these activities.

In 1908, the V.I.S. offered a prize for the best practical suggestion for community betterment. The winner was Harry W. Langworthy, the school principal, who broached a long-felt need—good sidewalks. Everyone complained about the terrible condition of the sidewalks along the main thoroughfares, and the ever-increasing automobile traffic made this improvement all the more imperative. The V.I.S. favored the idea, but was distressed to find, when construction began in 1911, that many old shade trees had to be removed; this issue was fiercely debated in the press.

About this time, a number of women from the upper village formed a sister group, the Canterbury Village Improvement Society. The two organizations, while retaining their separate identities, often worked together. Their first combined effort was a rummage sale for the St. Luke's Hospital fund; the next was a bazaar, one of many events to raise money for their crowning achievement—purchase of the Old Homestead, known today as the Sands-Ring House.

This venerable old structure had been the home of the Sands and Rings for almost one hundred and fifty years. The last family member to live there died in 1907, leaving a deteriorating building, smothered in unkempt shrubbery, which the two societies were determined to save. They launched a series of the inevitable benefits, the most notable being a series of concerts by the famous violinist David Mannes and his wife Clara, and a lecture by the naturalist Ernest Thompson Seton.

On January 4, 1912 came the announcement: "Purchase of the Ring Homestead" and the details: "Mrs. Lawrence F. Abbott and Mrs. William Applebye-Robinson attended the auction sale in Newburgh last Friday ... and purchased the property for the two organizations, by whom it will be jointly owned. The price was $2,000."

While the purchase funds were accumulating, the members discussed plans for the Old Homestead; it was "the only really old fashioned place in Cornwall" and they wanted to keep it that way. "The sentiment ... has been to preserve the place in its old time style of architecture so far as practicable, repairs to be made along those lines." After an assessment by architect Parker N. Hooper as to the extent of the renovations, Jaeger Brothers were hired for the work—to build a new foundation, a

13

new porch, walls and roof.

July 4, 1912 marked the official opening of the Old Homestead; two hundred people attended a reception at the restored house; the Firthcliffe Band performed, Rev. Lyman Abbott gave an address, and $150 was realized. In extolling the ladies on their great achievement, Rev. Abbott told about a men's improvement association which had accomplished little; an editorial in the 1879 newspaper had advised the men "to do more and say less."

In addition to preserving the Old Homestead for future generations, the societies intended to use it for the public benefit. One of the large rooms became a tearoom and Women's Exchange shop; another was the V.I.S. headquarters, and the third was rented for social gatherings. Two smaller rooms became kitchen and lavatory facilities. The societies now had to redouble their efforts in order to pay off the mortgage they had assumed for the repairs. The first donors in

response to an appeal for contributions were Thomas W. Weeks of Duncan Avenue, well-known for his philanthropy, and Mrs. Pauline Sands Lee,[4] a descendant of the Sands' family, who would be closely associated with the house in coming years.

While devoting energy and funds to the Old Homestead, each V.I.S. continued on its individual course, with tree planting, clean-up days, contests and other good works. When a new crusade came along—eradication of the house fly—young Eugene Previdi won the contest by catching 13,000 flies!

The Old Homestead prospered in its new role; visitors and social functions there were dutifully recorded by the *Cornwall Press*. A dance pavilion erected behind the house added to the popularity of the site as a community center. During World War I, the building served as headquarters for groups sending aid to war victims abroad.

February 12, 1992

The Brick Chapel

February is Black History Month—a fact which brings to mind the small brick church on Main Street which disappeared from the local scene only within the past twenty years. Modern residents remember the church as a dilapidated wreck set in an unkempt yard; a few may recall when it was in use, especially for the famous chicken suppers served by the church ladies.

The quaint little building underwent several transformations before it became the home of the Cornwall A.M.E. Zion congregation. Built around 1865 as a place of worship for local Catholics who had hitherto met in private homes, it stood originally on the north side of River Avenue, later across the street.

When the first congregation outgrew these quarters and left for a larger edifice on the present Hudson Street site, the smaller church became an Episcopalian Chapel where a Sunday school met and services were held, especially in the summer. Swedish families also came there to hear sermons in their native tongue.

In 1904 several black families formed a mission which met in a building at the corner of Cherry Avenue and Hudson Street. Then they organized into the Cornwall A.M.E. Zion Church, with a pastor, thirty-four charter members and a Sunday School of twenty. The next few years were busy ones as the small band labored earnestly to acquire a church of

---

4   Pauline Sands Lee (1864-1949) was the daughter of writer Edward Payson Roe and Anna Sands. She married Henry C. Lee and lived at their estate "Rock Acre" in Cornwall.

their own. First they raised money to buy a lot on Main Street near the Monument. Next came negotiations with Thomas Taft, then owner of the River Avenue chapel. He agreed to sell the building for $250.00 if the group would move it from his premises. Mr. Taft donated the first fifty dollars, and by the end of 1905, both the lot and building had been paid for, a feat accomplished by a variety of fund-raisers. There was a lecture on " The Educated Negro and the South of Today;" a fair; a stereopticon show by an ex-minister to Liberia; a concert featuring, among other talent, a three-year-old performer! The congregation met in the chapel until April. Then they dismantled the building and moved it, brick by brick, to the Main Street lot. In June they issued an appeal for community help in reaching the thousand dollars needed to erect the church. All they had were the windows and 29,000 bricks!

Another round of fund raising brought in enough money for contractor Harvey R. Taylor to proceed. The cornerstone was laid in September, 1907; and in January came the dedication—a day-long affair which included congratulatory remarks by fellow clergy.

At first the congregation was active, although it was a struggle to pay the pastor's salary and other on-going expenses. The community was generous; soon there was a small parsonage beside the church. The group pursued its modest course for a time until a number of factors led to decline: a new mobility brought about by the automobile; a lack of job opportunities, and a postwar shift in population.

In the 1970s the church again became newsworthy, not because of a resurgence, but due to the dangerous condition of the decaying structure. Pictures reveal gaping windows, a hanging door, a littered interior. For almost a decade thereafter, items in *The Local* record attempts by the town to have the building renovated or razed. The Zion Church of Newburgh now owned the property and indicated an interest in saving the church, as did historically-minded Cornwallites, but nothing came of these efforts. Finally the parsonage was torn down, the church roof caved in and was removed, and one day, the building was gone.

February 27, 1991

Firth Carpet Company

The history of the Firth Carpet Company— Cornwall's leading industry for over half a century—deserves to be recalled and preserved as an important segment of town history. This brief review is based on the files of *The Cornwall Local*, old histories, and interviews with former Firth employees.

When Lewis Beach published his book on Cornwall in 1873, the site of the future Firth Carpet Company was occupied by another plant, the Cornwall Woolen Mills, owned by F.W. Broadhead, whom Beach described as "a gentleman of long and varied experience in the manufacture of woolens." He employed about one hundred and twenty-five men, women, and children. The first structure on the site, however, had been the Townsend Cotton Factory, built in 1812, which was in operation until a fire destroyed the works.

Broadhead's mill stood on the banks of Moodna Creek, from which it derived some of its power. E.M. Ruttenber, a 19th-century historian, described the plant in some detail: the various machines on its four floors and the daily output in yards of cloth. Perhaps a fire discouraged the owner, for early in the 1880s, the property was for sale.

The Firth Carpet Company was a division of T.F. Firth and Sons, a well-known rug manufacturing firm located in Yorkshire, England. In 1884 a branch was established in Philadelphia and, two years later, the Broadhead property in Cornwall was purchased. An article from an early issue of *The Cornwall Local* states: "At that time the mills proper were surrounded by a dense growth of trees and undergrowth ... [They] had been unoccupied for four years, and were in an extremely

15

dilapidated condition," requiring extensive renovation. By the fall of 1886 the plant was ready to begin the manufacture of yarn, followed in the spring by a weaving department. The firm was organized as Firth Carpet Company with Thomas F. Firth, president; Algernon F. Firth, vice president; Bennet H. Tobey, treasurer; and Fred Booth, secretary. The American headquarters was in New York City.

Twelve years after its founding in Cornwall, three hundred workers were on the payroll and the company boasted of making "strong efforts to furnish steady employment to its hands at good wages," pointing out that in the panic of 1893, Firth had remained open when other carpet mills in the country were shut down. During these first years, new buildings were added, also a 500-horse power Corliss engine and a large water wheel, both to generate power. When the plant was "electrified," five hundred 20-candlepower lights were installed. Under the supervision of James H. Aspinall, a three-story brick building (52 x 150 feet) was erected in 1899.

An article of 1900 explains the process of making tapestry Brussels carpets as carried on at Firth. After sorting, the raw wool was washed, then blown through a pipe to the carding room, where it was spun into yarn. Washed and bleached, the yarn went to the printing room where the color was added; then steamed to make it color fast. Washed again and dried in huge drying machines, the yarn was wound on bobbins and sent to the weaving department. By 1900 three hundred and fifty workers were producing 450 rolls of carpet per year.

Thomas F. Firth (later Sir Thomas) kept abreast of the operations on this side of the Atlantic through the annual trips made by his son Algernon. Both men were held in great respect, for they both had a life-long experience in the carpet industry. Some of the Cornwall workers had also started in the Firth plant in England before emigrating to America. Fred Booth, the superintendent, had gone to work at thirteen before coming to America in 1886. Many of the Firth workers were described as "men well educated and well read, who take pride in the quality of their work."

The Cornwall area where the Firth Carpet Company was located had its name changed from Montana to West Cornwall; then, appropriately, to Firthcliffe; and Montana Drive became known as Mill Street. It was a close-knit community, dominated by the mill — with its own railroad station, post office, primary school, stores, barber shop and chapel. A British-American Association flourished, for ties with the old country were strong; a cherished dream for many a Firth employee was to save up for a trip "home."

In the decades before World War I, as first-generation workers were replaced by their children, Firth Carpet Company continued to expand under superintendent Fred Booth and his successor, Morris M. Davidson. In addition to new buildings at the plant, the firm purchased forty acres and erected single and two-family houses on Mill, Algernon and Firth Streets, which were rented to the workers. A clubhouse (burned down in 1970) was termed "a princely gift;" it contained bowling alleys, billiard room, gymnasium, library and other recreational facilities. The company sponsored a baseball team which played on a field also the site of the first annual outings. There was also a Firth Carpet Company Band which performed in a bandstand near the club.

As Sir Algernon Firth followed in his father's footsteps, the fortunes of the company fluctuated with the prevailing economic climate. When times were good, the number of employees escalated and bonuses were offered. When the rug market was depressed, people were laid off, wages and hours reduced; and sometimes a strike would be called. The weavers struck in 1907, demanding a 15% wage increase; as a result, the mill shut down for three months —, "probably the greatest calamity that ever visited Cornwall, affecting every line of business," commented *The Local*. Credit for settling the strike went to Father Brosnan of St. Thomas Church. As a large number of the strikers were his parishioners, "he was given full authority to act for them" and was able to negotiate a settlement; after which the management declared that every effort would be made to regain the markets lost during the strike.

Business soared during World War I as the firm undertook war contracts of woolen goods and haversack cloth. Firth led the com-

16

munity in contributions to the Liberty Fund Drives and many of its employees saw war service, a few joining British and Canadian regiments. When the Firth Clubhouse was enlarged in 1919, it was dedicated to the Firthcliffe veterans of World War I.

September 21, 1994

Mead and Taft Company

The names of Mead and Taft are familiar to anyone who knows about Cornwall history. Many people can recall the firm's large brick building at the Landing — across from the railroad station, on the site of today's riverfront park. There are families in town whose relatives once worked for Mead and Taft and remember a time when the firm was not only prominent in the construction business, but was also an important part of the town's economy.

The story begins with Daniel Taft, who came to Cornwall around 1837. A few years later he went into the carpentry business in a building near the Sands-Ring House where he could utilize the waterpower of Canterbury Creek. Around 1857 he moved to a house he had bought on River Avenue and erected a shop on the grounds. Here the power was produced "by horses pulling a sweep around in a circle." The final move in 1866 was to a frame building at the Landing. By this time his son Thomas had returned from the Civil War and, after a short interval in New York, joined the firm. Mead and Taft Company was now a partnership of Charles H. Mead and his brother-in-law Thomas Taft, with Daniel as foreman, a post he retained until his retirement when he was seventy-eight years old.

The factory at the Landing was destroyed by a fire in the 1870s, but was immediately replaced with a three-story building of brick. The business expanded rapidly as Mead and Taft sought contracts outside the local area. Hotels and cottages were built at Long Branch, New Jersey; a hotel at Montauk, Long Island; an orphanage at Sparkill; buildings at St. Stephen's College, Barrytown; a portion of the Mohonk Mountain House; and several buildings at Millbrook, including the huge Halcyon Hall Hotel. By 1892 there were four hundred and fifty people on the payroll and the firm had established an office at Tuxedo Park, where they would construct many of the luxurious summer homes. The dock at the factory was enlarged for the firm's schooner, the *Emily Irene*, which delivered building materials to sites along the river and further afield. Thomas Taft patented an award-winning prefabricated building. A large quantity were sold to the British government for use in the West Indies; one was even shipped to Istanbul.

The Mead and Taft ad appeared each week in *The Local*. In addition to building activities, "the firm deals extensively in lumber, coal and builders' supplies of all description and also conducts a real estate business." A hardware store sold paint, seed, tools, and fertilizer as well as lumber. The firm's far-flung business was impressive: a number of carpenters worked at the Cornwall plant, fashioning the hardwood mantels, panelling and fine wood carving in which they specialized. But most of the six hundred workmen were employed on the various building contracts. Over the years the company paid out "millions of dollars to Cornwall people."

After the death of Charles H. Mead in 1905, James T. Howell joined the firm and, for a brief period, the name was changed to The Taft Howell Company. "After a year Mr. Howell decided that he did not like the building business and sold his stock to Mr. Taft;" the original name was then resumed with Taft as head of the firm. In March 1911 another fire destroyed much of the plant, but by setting up a temporary office nearby and rebuilding as rapidly as possible, the company was able to continue in business. "The ensuing years were busy ones as the Company was fortunate in securing many large contracts...."

Thomas' son, Thomas K., took over at the death of his father in 1920. "From then until

17

the depression of 1929," he later recalled, "the Company was very busy. Work at Tuxedo continued in good volume," and large houses were built in New Windsor, Goshen and Dutchess County. In an effort to keep the shop working at capacity, the carpenters made such items as directory boards for hotel lobbies, two thousand display cases for the Du Pont Company, and pieces for designers of modern furniture.

Our chief interest today lies in the houses built by Mead and Taft in Cornwall. Unfortunately the list is far from complete, and many of the buildings have not survived. One of the first projects with which Thomas Taft, Sr. was concerned was the Mountain House, an immense hotel on the site later occupied by Dr. Ernest G. Stillman's summer home — he de-

signed the pavilion, a unique feature of the hotel. Mead and Taft built at least two houses on Duncan Avenue: the large rambling home of James Stillman, now Jogue's Retreat, and the neighboring "Marble Palace" for Mrs. Anna R. Gazzam, now gone. On the mountain the firm built part of Storm King School's Main Building and a house for Dr. Edward L. Partridge — both gone; but one of the "cottages" built for the Storm King Club on Deer Hill Road still stands. Some of the Matthiessen Park houses are their work, also the Santoro building which stood in the Village Square, and Red Men's Hall.

April 11, 1993
April 28, 1993
May 5, 1993

Cocks' Store

In the days before supermarkets and shopping malls, people used to shop at local stores, often within walking distance of their homes. Along Cornwall's Main and Hudson Streets could be found all sorts of stores: groceries and bakeries, meat and fish markets, stores selling clothing, shoes, hardware, harness and feed; pharmacies, tobacco, newspaper and confectionery shops; and before Cornwall went "dry," a number of saloons. One of the oldest of these business places was the Cocks' Grocery Store, located at the corner of Hudson Street and Cherry Avenue — now the Butter Hill Antique Shop. Some history about the store and the family who operated it for one hundred and twenty years will interest former customers as well as those who have come to Cornwall after the store's demise.

In 1950 Cocks' Store celebrated its 100th anniversary, for which *The Local* published a special edition. Two of the founder's sons were then living; from their memories which spanned a lifetime's work at the store came a rich collection of reminiscences. It was in 1850 that Charles E. Cocks opened a grocery store at Cornwall Landing; he was then twenty-eight years old, and exchanged a career of school teacher for that of grocer. His business prospered, for the Landing was then

a populous community, and his appointment as postmaster brought in additional customers. When Cornwall became a thriving summer resort, Charles E. met the demands of the lucrative boarding house trade by moving his store uptown to the corner of Cherry and Hudson. He already owned a small farm nearby where he raised fruits and vegetables for sale at the store; the surplus was shipped to New York. Charles E. had a large family — the girls helped with the summer boarders at their home and picked the garden produce. The boys did the heavier farm chores, and everyone worked at the store which was open from 6 A.M. to 9 P.M. and until 11 on Saturday nights. Old pictures show that the store was quite small at first, but was enlarged over the years to the present dimensions. Additional buildings were erected: a barn, stable, and an ice house. During the early years, Charles E. had a succession of partners; his son Charles C. joined the firm in 1880, followed twelve years later by his brother Isaac M. However, the store was a family affair, and both boys had worked there from an early age. Their sister Hannah kept the books; she had returned to school for a postgraduate course in bookkeeping. After the founder retired in 1899, his two sons were well prepared to carry on the business. They were joined in 1908 by Charles C.'s son, William B. Cocks, and later two more family members came into the firm: Isaac's son, Anthony R., and William B.'s son, Charles II.

When interviewed by *The Local* in 1950, the Cocks family had many stories to relate. They told how Charles C. had started the country route in the 1880s. He would leave the store early in the morning and sometimes make as many as sixty-five stops — buying eggs and butter from the farmers and selling them products from the store. "Business on the routes became so heavy that it was necessary to put on teams of horses with two men to handle the huge loads: barrels of sugar, tubs of butter, and to pick up the tremendous quantity of eggs running as high as 400 dozen on a trip .... It was expensive to operate the delivery routes... The wagons were made especially for the country trips with removable boxes and compartments and shelves for sugar, spices, coffee and tea." One of the duties of the night watchman was to keep the wagon stocked with groceries.

In the early days, one of the Cocks brothers would make a weekly trip to New York to purchase items for the store, often taking a member of the next generation to be trained in this aspect of the business. Flour came from the West by the carload, potatoes direct from Maine. They bought their coffee green and roasted it each week, at first by hand — the price, five pounds for a dollar. Charles C. traveled to Delaware County where the best butter could be obtained — it was shipped in 100-pound firkins. Cheese, half a ton at a time, came from Herkimer County. Sugar was sold in 100-pound bags, or larger amounts.

The store changed over the years to keep pace with the times. Early accounts were kept in huge ledgers, a cumbersome method, especially when recording large orders. Later, each customer was issued a passbook in which purchases were recorded and the bill paid monthly. Old timers will remember when a clerk would call at one's home to solicit orders, which were delivered the same day. Or one could phone in an order — the store had two telephone lines. Plate glass replaced the original windows; modern cases improved the cluttered appearance of an earlier period. In 1930 the store added a case for Birdseye Frosted Foods — the first store in the Hudson Valley to do so. A meat market opened in 1948 and two years later the store was converted to a self-service market. But throughout the years, two items remained unchanged. The first was "a novel device" by which a clerk anywhere in the store could reach up and pull a cord to open the door for customers leaving the store laden with parcels. The second was the advertisements which had appeared ever since the town had a newspaper. They, too, were unique — chatty messages as though from a friend who had inside information to impart on the best buys of the week.

For one hundred and twenty years, Cocks' Store was a part of Cornwall history, touching the lives of hundreds of townspeople — generations of customers as well as the people employed there over the years.

December 2, 1992

The Masonic Temple

A few years ago the relative of a Main Street businessman conceived the idea of compiling a history of Main Street by researching the builder and date of each structure, and listing all the different businesses which had been housed in each. An ambitious project, but impossible to accomplish, as he soon discovered. Complex property transactions, old maps, pictures and newspaper items, conflicting statements by old sources and modern owners produced a bewildering mass of data which confirmed only one fact — that change is implicit in community development!

A general overview of Main Street can be traced, and some of the buildings can be documented accurately; but fires, demolition and renovations have obscured the history of many other properties. By the early 1800s, the large tracts held by the first settlers — Sands,

19

Carpenter, Thorn and Townsend — were being subdivided, and the portions along Main Street, laid out in small lots, were being purchased by such entrepreneurs as Thomas Fish, the Chadeayne family and Ebenezer Sutherland.

From early times, the intersection of Main Street and Willow Avenue was an important corner. Before the town of Cornwall existed, the north side was the site of the Nathaniel Sands farmhouse; his son David later moved into a nearby dwelling, the Sands-Ring House. In those days, Main Street probably contained few other houses.

The opposite corner (242-244 Main Street) was not developed until the next century. In 1882 James M. Smith had a drug store and residence there. Thirteen years later, Artemas C. and George B. Case moved their grocery store into this building. A picture of the Case establishment shows wide, shallow steps across the front, protected by a roof with a balcony above.

The next structure to occupy the site was the present large concrete block building erected by the Cornwall Industrial Corporation around 1920. This commercial enterprise was the brainchild of Dr. Ernest G. Stillman, a brother of Charles Chauncey Stillman of Kenridge Farm. Its purpose was to provide job opportunities in the post-World War I economy. Five existing businesses were merged into a single entity: the Cornwall Hardware Store, the Harvey R. Taylor Construction Company (located behind the new building), the Black Rock Realty Company, the Forge Hill Ice Company and the *Cornwall Press*, the town newspaper.

After purchasing the paper from editor L. G. Goodnough, the group used the *Cornwall Press* office next to the Cornwall Presbyterian Church for their quarters until the Main Street facility was built. When new, this building contained high windows on both the Main Street and Willow Avenue sides, providing light and ventilation for the corporation offices, the printing establishment and hardware store.

The newspapers of 1921 carried ads by the various departments: "We are now ready to construct buildings of all kinds and to do general repairing," stated one. Another urged:

"Add to the beauty of your home. Let us build you a beautiful artistic pergola." "Your last chance to build a new six-room cottage in Cornwall," declared a Realty Company ad. These "cottages" were located in Highland View Park, a 250-acre tract between Willow Avenue and the present hospital, which was being developed by the corporation. Several of these houses can still be seen on Grand and Chestnut Streets — square in shape, with a porch across the front and a row of dormer windows above. The construction department had secured two other contracts: the Cornwall-on-Hudson High School and the Butterfield Memorial Library in Cold Spring.

The Corporation printed an illustrated brochure which detailed the potential of the new enterprise in glowing terms. "The Construction Department ... is complete in every detail ... from the raw lumber to the finished building" and employed a staff of skilled workmen. The Realty Company proposed that a group of people intending to build form an association and "submit their desires," after which the company will prepare plans and estimates. By erecting several houses, substantial savings can be effected. The ice plant manufactured artificial ice from the pure water of an artesian well, supplanting the former practice of harvesting ice from the Hudson River, even then polluted. "The Warehouses of the Hardware Department ... are stocked with everything for building construction, agricultural equipment and household hardware;" harness and other leather products are a specialty. "The printing department is developing into one of the largest and most up-to-date ... establishments in Orange County .... equipped to handle any job of printing..." This department published the *Cornwall Press*, a newspaper "designed for the American home," according to the editor, Creswell Maclaughlin. The same telephone number — Cornwall 300 — served all departments.

By 1923, the group had built another large structure near the river, on the Shore Road site of an old brickyard. Most of the operations were transferred there, but the Cornwall Industrial Corporation was a short-lived venture; by 1927 it had been dissolved except for the printing plant which, under the name of

The Cornwall Press, Inc., continued for several decades, employing many local residents in the business of printing books. The building now houses the East Coast Theatre Supply Company, which makes stage sets for theatrical productions.

When the building on Main Street became vacant, it was taken over by the Jerusalem Temple Lodge of Masons and the Order of Eastern Stars. Known for many years as the Masonic Temple, it served as a meeting place for the two groups as well as for large community gatherings. After the Masons and the Eastern Stars moved to the Grange Hall in Mountainville, the building was altered to suit other tenants: Cornwall Ceramics for a time, and the Hudson Valley Gymnastics School. A recent addition is a children's clothing store.

Many people have undoubtedly wondered about this odd-looking building in the center of Main Street; its seventy-year history has been a varied one: corporate offices, printing press, meeting rooms, gymnasium and stores.

December 11, 1991

The Riverfront Park

Not long ago, an old timer was heard to remark that the park at the riverfront was one of the best things that had ever happened in Cornwall, and many of the regular park habitués might agree.

This broad, green expanse along the river, dotted with growing shade trees, has a two-fold function. The first is recreational — a place for picnics, boating, fishing, sun bathing, or just relaxing — all in an unsurpassed scenic setting. The second purpose is a far-reaching one: to preserve this section of the Hudson River shoreline from the depredation of commercial development.

Cornwall Landing was not always a stretch of greenway. The senior citizen who sang the praises of the park can remember a very different scene. Where people now launch their pleasure craft, the *Mary Powell* and other river steamers used to dock; and adjacent to the railroad tracks stood the depot serving the West Shore and the Ontario and Western Railroads — both dock and depot busy with the arrival and departure of passengers and freight. Where the grassy carpet now stretches along the shore, a three-story brick building once stood, housing the offices, hardware store and workshops of Mead and Taft Company, a long-established firm of building contractors.

The forebears of our park lover lived at Cornwall Landing, in those days a thriving community. An old directory lists some of the business places in 1885: boarding-houses, two small hotels, a saloon, Nathan Clark's general store, Reuben Clark's coal and feed store, Seaman's grocery, a bakery, two shoe and boot shops, a post office, agents for the American Express and the National Express (before the days of parcel post), and the Mead and Taft plant. There was also a small Quaker chapel (still standing on the Yacht Club grounds), which was used for a Sunday School. A number of families had their homes in the vicinity of these businesses. But the most important features of the Landing were the docks and railroad facilities.

It is hard to imagine the scene on a summer weekend when a vast assemblage of horse-drawn vehicles would congregate at the Landing to meet the throngs of visitors arriving by boat or train, bound for the many hotels and boarding houses in town. These were the years when Cornwall was a popular summer resort.

Then began a gradual decline in this once busy settlement, which accelerated in the past fifty years. First the boat traffic ceased, then the passenger trains stopped running. A fire destroyed the Mead and Taft factory. The small business places closed and most of the residents moved elsewhere. The final chapter was the arrival of Con Ed in the early sixties, with plans to construct a pumped storage hydroelectric plant at the base of Storm King Mountain. While waiting for a license to proceed, the utility acquired most of Cornwall Landing, demolished the existing buildings, and modified the terrain to fit its requirements. After the construction was blocked by one

21

court order after another, the project was finally abandoned.

Cornwall-on-Hudson, although losing part of the village, was the beneficiary in the form of the new park, created in part from landfill removed from the Con Ed construction site. This parkland was given to the village by Con Ed and in September, 1992 was named the Michael J. Donahue Memorial Park for the village mayor whose twenty-year tenure had been dominated by the Con Ed controversy.

July 12, 1993

EVENTS

These articles include several note-worthy happenings of the early 20th century, beginning with Cornwall's part in the Hudson-Fulton Commemoration of 1909. This was a one-day celebration, preceded by months of planning. Other occurrences lasted for several years, as when the Catskill Aqueduct was constructed beneath the town and when the Storm King Highway was built. The first World War also had a noticeable impact on the town, especially the period of America's participation. Other articles describe some typical events: a school graduation, a Fourth of July Celebration, an annual summer picnic. And the section ends with a memorable occasion — the opening of The Cornwall Hospital. Parades took place with great frequency, for this mode of celebration could involve any number of participants and also provide an acceptable outlet for jubilation.

The Hudson-Fulton Celebration

The Handy Guide to the Hudson River and Catskill Mountains, published by Rand McNally, can be found today in old book catalogues, priced far beyond the original cost of twenty-five cents. The 1909 Hudson-Fulton Celebration edition is of special interest. A preview of the commemoration is outlined in the preface: "The Fall of 1909 will witness the striking and joint celebration of Hendrick Hudson's discovery of the Hudson River three hundred years ago and of Robert Fulton's epoch-making experiment in steam navigation in 1807. Imposing observances, religious, musical, literary, historical, military and naval will mark the occasion and the whole Hudson Valley will participate."

Cornwall's part in the Hudson-Fulton Celebration of 1909 is the subject of this article. Early in February *The Cornwall Press* wrote that plans for the festival were progressing under the direction of the Upper Hudson Counties Commission, comprising governing officials of communities along the river. To help fund the celebration, a bill for $300,000 was introduced in the state legislature; a second bill is noteworthy in that it called for the preservation of the Hudson Highlands. An-

other newspaper article mentioned that a replica of Hudson's *Half Moon* was under construction in the Netherlands and Fulton's *Clermont* was being duplicated by Staten Island shipbuilders — an exact replica except for safety measures required by modern steamboat inspection regulations.

The Cornwall Hudson-Fulton Committee was so plagued by acrimony and friction it is a wonder that any celebration was held at all. Should the town supervisor or the village mayor head the committee? Mayor John Clarkson seems to have assumed the role of chairman. His diplomatic gesture of appointing people from "outside the village" was hotly criticized by those who reasoned that, since the village bordered on the Hudson River, village residents should have the sole right to serve on the committee. However, it was Clarkson's appointment of a villager which occasioned the greatest controversy — his choice of Creswell Maclaughlin as secretary. Maclaughlin was publicly castigated as "Cornwall's most undesirable citizen." In his role as public speaker and newspaper man, he deliberately gibed at the "establishment" and this ridicule did not sit well with those entrenched in public office. When several of the committee resigned in protest, one of its leading members, Col. Sebastian C. Jones, superintendent of the New York Military Academy, tried to act as peacemaker. In a letter to the newspaper, he berated Cornwall for sitting back "sullen, discontented and uninterested instead of doing its share in behalf of the greatest historical pageant and festival the world has ever seen." Maclaughlin, refusing to resign, had worked faithfully, said Jones. "Why not let it go at that and all pull together to give the children ... the biggest day they have ever dreamed of." The committee was doing its best in a difficult situation and needed the support of the community.

The two-week-long celebration began on September 25th in New York City where the *Half Moon* and *Clermont* were on view in the harbor. The rest of the week was filled with the pageants, parades, banquets, carnivals, fireworks and other observances foretold in the Guidebook. On October 1st the two ships, escorted by a flotilla of vessels, started up the Hudson, and the remainder of the second week was devoted to observances by communities along the river.

Cornwall's celebration came on Friday, October 3rd. The local committee had previously advertised for refreshment, souvenir and other concessions, and sought accommodations for visitors. Druggist Henry N. Clark ran an ad for Hudson-Fulton souvenirs. On Friday morning, a parade marched along Main and Hudson Streets to end at Palmer's Park (now Cliffside), where one could get a fine view of the *Half Moon* and the *Clermont* in the bay. The committee had assembled an impressive number of units — the parade was headed by the Catskill Aqueduct police (then on duty in town), marshals Charles Jaeger (village) and Edward L. Sylcox (town), and Civil War veterans riding in open carriages. Then came the N.Y.M.A. band and corps of cadets, followed by the village trustees (no mention of the town board) and students from the Cornwall schools. The fraternal lodges entered floats as did some of the merchants. The Highland Engine Company transported its original pumper "Young America" and the Storm King firemen also displayed some of their apparatus.

In the afternoon, many people went to Newburgh to witness the huge military parade, the evening fireworks and illumination of the vessels in the river. Others stayed in Cornwall for an afternoon program or boarded a launch which "took passengers out for a little sail around the two boats.... Numerous craft were in the waters and the harbor presented a beautiful sight."

As a final gesture, the Cornwall committee had erected a sign on Palmer's Knoll— "large letters... illuminated with electric lights brought out the name Cornwall into handsome prominence, while a nice display of fireworks added to the pleasure of the evening." So despite the dissension in the ranks, the committee's Hudson-Fulton effort was satisfactory, if not outstanding.

September 29, 1993

The Businessmen's Picnic

In the early decades of the present century, the Cornwall Businessmen's Picnic was the high point of the summer season. There were other events: fairs, strawberry festivals, bandstand concerts, and similar entertainments, but measured in attendance, the picnic surpassed all these lesser attractions. Artemas C. Case, a Canterbury merchant, was the founder.

The first picnic was held in 1904. A notice of the projected event appeared in late July:

"A meeting has been called for Monday evening, August 1, at 8 p.m. at the store of A.C. and G.B. Case to discuss plans for a Businessmen's picnic... It is hoped that arrangements can be perfected whereby the business people in general... can participate in a thoroughly enjoyable outing." Plans matured, committees were appointed, Dr. W.W. Page of St. John's Church named chairman, and contributions solicited.

Most of the town stores closed on August 24th, the day of the picnic. By nine o'clock in the morning, a crowd had started to gather on the Storm King golf course, the site of the festivities. The first event was a baseball game between the two villages. The fact that most of the participants had not played in years made for much hilarity and good-natured ribbing. After the noon-day meal came athletic contests and music by the Firthcliffe Band. Throughout the day, soft drinks, ice cream and peanuts could be purchased from Toombs and Barton, who had the refreshment concession. Comments from some of the estimated crowd of two thousand augured well for a repeat performance. The picnic became an annual event.

In 1907 the affair drew an even larger crowd. That year, the two fire companies competed in the baseball game, Storm King Engine defeating Highland Engine by 16-13. A regular refreshment stand served lunch to those who had not brought their own. A platform had been erected, from which the speakers addressed the audience and the Village Band performed. After the usual athletic contests, there were two innovations. The first was a parade of hack drivers, an idea proposed by Chauncey Stillman, who offered a twenty-dollar prize for the best one-horse hack and ten dollars for second prize. "There were eight entries from five different stables. The horses were walked up the course and trotted back." Reported the paper: "The vehicles were spic and span, the horses shone in glistening coats, robes and harness were in fine condition and the drivers neatness personified." The judges awarded the first prize to Walter Wood, the second to Walter Davis.

Next came the Balloon Ascension, "the best drawing card of the day." After an unsuccessful first attempt, the balloon soared aloft, "the daring young aeronaut" swinging from a trapeze underneath. At a height of between fifteen hundred and two thousand feet, "the parachute was cut loose and after a little drop through space, opened beautifully, carrying the performer gracefully downward .... The parachute and its passenger landed a short distance away from the picnic grounds, beyond the road next to the golf links." The same stunt was repeated the following year.

The 1909 picnic was held in September to coincide with the Hudson-Fulton Celebration and the site moved to the estate overlooking the river, now Cliffside Park. In 1915 there was a real departure from tradition. Over the strong objections of a vocal minority, it was decided to hold the picnic at the new Bear Mountain Park. August 19th was a cool, crystal-clear day, and early in the morning, Hudson Street was thronged with picnickers making their way to Cornwall Landing to board the *Albany* for the sail to Bear Mountain. Here, on the level plain near the lake, the customary events took place—a ballgame organized by Grant Clark, music by the sixteen-member Cornwall Band, exercises in the pavilion at which the Honorable George W. Perkins, president of the Palisades Park Commission, addressed the gathering. Boating on the lake and patronizing the lunch counter in the headquarters building were popular diversions.

Concluded the *Cornwall-Press*: "Although many were lukewarm with respect to the innovation of holding the Businessmen's Picnic at Bear Mountain, the large number who attended are enthusiastic in their praise." Among these enthusiasts were Thomas Taft and his son, A. C. Case (originator of the picnic), Dr. W. W. Page (the perennial chairman), Town Supervisor Charles J. Jaeger and Town Clerk Charles E. Mailler, Principal H. W. Langworthy and forty guests from the Blind Home.

The war years put an end to this annual event; it would not be revived until years later as the Lions Club Cornwall Community Day.

August 14, 1991

Fires

Fire fighting in olden times was a frustrating and thankless job. With primitive equipment, inadequate water supply, insufficient pressure, and maddeningly slow methods of transportation, the firemen often arrived to find the building entirely consumed, and could only do their best to keep the fire from spreading to nearby structures. During the 150-year history of the local fire departments, there have been a good many fires in Cornwall: barns or other outbuildings, houses and business places, and forest fires in the surrounding mountains. Here are three of the most spectacular fires of the early 20th century.

The N.Y.M.A. fire of January 1910 resulted in a terrible tragedy, the loss of the school's main building. The structure had formerly been a grand hotel, the Glen Ridge House — three hundred feet long, four stories high, with a long porch across the front. After standing empty for some years, it had become the New York Military Academy in 1889.

The fire was discovered about 2:30 A.M. by one of the cadets. Smelling smoke, he went to investigate and found the servants' stairway ablaze. Fire call was sounded on the bugle and the building evacuated of its two hundred occupants in exemplary fashion. The village fire alarm rang at 2:45, and by 3:10 the Storm King firemen had arrived - "a half mile from the village over snowy roads"; Highland Engine was also called out. The fact that sixteen hundred feet of hose had to be stretched up the slope from the nearest hydrant so lessened the water pressure "that its effectiveness was to a great extent lost." "With a tremendous crash and flare of flames visible for miles, the roof fell in, and the building burned to the ground within an hour." The student body's "ready response to all orders" prevented any fatalities. After the boys assembled for roll call on the lawn, the acting commandant returned to the building to search every room; "his singed hair and eyebrows bear witness to this really heroic deed."

The firemen's chagrin at being unable to save the building is evident in the following report: "Had there been a hydrant near at hand, there is little doubt that the fire could have been put out with slight damage, as it was nearly manageable at first, and several times, those who were so pluckily fighting it, thought they had it under control; but burning from one floor to another, up the long stairway, which ran from basement to upper floor, it gained such headway that only a heavy stream of water promptly applied, could have extinguished the flames."

The boys were lodged for the rest of the night in adjacent homes; early the next morning, the superintendent, Colonel S.C. Jones, rented the unoccupied Elmer House, and the adjoining Grand View House for the remainder of the school year. By February, plans were underway for a new N.Y.M.A.

A year after this fire, *The Cornwall Local* of March 30, 1911 carried a report of another disaster—a fire at Mead and Taft Company's plant— described as "the severest blow to Cornwall in many a year." The fire started in a shed, supposedly struck by lightning during a thunderstorm, and it had smoldered until fanned into flames by strong winds. The engineer of a passing train noticed the blaze and turned in the alarm. All of the local fire companies responded; Storm King, being closest, arrived first, their apparatus pulled by a team from Lewis Brothers' stable, next door to the firehouse. Many readers will remember William B. Cocks, the Storm King foreman in charge of fighting the fire. One company started out from Newburgh; when their cart became mired in the mud, the crew abandoned it and proceeded to the fire by auto. The firemen "worked in extreme peril much of the time," but could make little headway against the fire which was spread by the strong winds throughout the three-story building.

At that time, Mead and Taft had about three hundred and fifty men in its employ, many of whom were local residents. Their jobs were gone and many lost valuable tools in the fire. Commented *The Local*: "There are few houses in Cornwall that do not feel the Mead and Taft loss a personal one." But the paper voiced the confidence "... that the same energy and ability which has reared this great industry will rebuild it on the foundations of the old." The impact on the local economy was severe but of short duration. The firm rented quarters in several adjacent buildings and carried on in this fashion until the erection of a new building.

"Fire Causes $80,000 Damage To Cornwall Garage" blared a headline in *The Local* of January 28, 1926 — "the most disastrous fire in years." The blaze had broken out on a Sunday morning. When the intense heat knocked out the alarm system by melting the telephone cables, the church bells were rung, but on a Sunday morning, no one paid any attention. The Highland Engine firehouse was just a block away, but by the time the firemen assembled, the fire had spread so rapidly that within half an hour the building was in ruins. When a beam collapsed or a wall caved in, great showers of sparks rose and lit on the adjoining wooden houses. The fire fighters turned their attention to saving these structures and received the gratitude of Main Street merchants for their successful efforts.

The cause of the fire was thought to be an exploding furnace. The flames came into contact with a vat of oil and spread quickly into the main section of the garage. "Volumes of smoke and flames would shoot high into the air" as the fire came in contact with the gas tanks of the cars stored there. Of the thirty-six cars in the garage at the time of the fire, only one was saved. Some of the cars were new, others belonged to the townspeople: Dr. E.G. Stillman's Lafayette, J. Edwin Knapp's Ford sedan, T.W. Weeks' Packard. The Cornwall Garage had been modernized in 1917, its wooden walls replaced by a brick exterior. The owner, Harry E. Keevill, was an enterprising young man and a foreman of the Highland Engine Company. A measure of his popularity is the following notice: "Fellow citizens to clean up garage ruins Saturday. Keep the smile on Harry's face, boys! Several merchants and townsmen have enlisted." Later, a Main Street businessman, grateful that his store had been spared, contributed a generous sum toward the installation of a better alarm system. And Keevill rebuilt his garage, which still stands on the west side of Main Street not far from Willow Avenue.

May 6, 13, 1992

The Catskill Aqueduct, I

A discussion of drinking water in last week's article leads naturally to a further consideration of the topic — not Cornwall's water supply this time, but New York City's, which flows through a gigantic pipe beneath the town.

A statement in the 1976 booklet on Cornwall reads: "Can you imagine a construction job almost going unnoticed while it cost more than three million dollars, employed hundreds of men and lasted almost four years? Such was the case when one of the engineering marvels of its time passed through Cornwall." Not so. Anyone who studies the newspapers of 1909-1914 cannot fail to realize that the Catskill Aqueduct had a definite impact on Cornwall, even though most of the construction was invisible.

The huge undertaking—that of bringing water from the Catskill Mountains to New York City—was front page news. And when teams arrived in Cornwall to survey the route, the project acquired an immediacy, strengthened by the lengthy process of land condemnation. How could a property owner in the throes of litigation over selling land to the New York City Board of Water Supply be unaware of the project? From a list of some twenty owners whose land was taken, the route of the aqueduct could be ascertained. The pipeline would enter the town in Firthcliffe, cross under the present high school to the former Blind Home; from there to Duncan Avenue, then to Round Top; and crossing Mountain Road, continue along the flank of Storm King Mountain to the Hudson River.

Work on the Cornwall sector began in 1909; by 1911 about fifteen hundred workers were employed on the job, most of them migrant laborers. Evidence that work was in progress could be seen in the buildings erected at the sites of the various shafts and in the local housing shortage. "There is a growing demand for vacant houses in this end of the village," stated *The Local*. It was due mostly to the influx of aqueduct workmen, "a number of whom intend to remain here at least four years."

The white collar workers with families rented houses, while the single men lived in boarding houses, which could look forward to good business for the next several years. For the actual construction work, the contractor brought in crews of Greeks, Hungarians, Poles and blacks, most of whom were housed in rough shacks clustered near the shafts in Firthcliffe and at the end of Bay View Avenue. Some workers took apartments in town; the former Barton and Spooner building on lower Duncan Avenue, then vacant, became the abode of an undesirable element, "the Bee Hive," people called it, and the police kept an eye on it. This sudden increase in population, although temporary, caused overcrowding in the schools, especially in Cornwall-on-Hudson, where some classrooms had forty pupils.

In addition to housing, other structures were needed. The main aqueduct office was located on River Avenue in what would later become the Village Office; the superintendent lived in the Carley mansion nearby. The greatest concentration of buildings was on Bay View Avenue near the future Storm King Highway; here were workmen's shacks, commissary and dining quarters, storage sheds, compressor plant and engineer's house. The Josiah Clark home was turned into a hospital. The police force of thirty men had its headquarters near the Catholic Church; the men lived across from the present Town Hall and stabled their horses in a barn on the Blind Home property.

Although the bulk of the excavating and tunneling was done by migrant labor, many local men found work, especially as engineers, clerks, in transportation or supplies. One example was blacksmith Michael Fogarty, who was kept busy shoeing the horses and mules. The town profited in other ways, too. Mead and Taft Company erected the compressor building, and the Clark dock was leased for the aqueduct boat to land with supplies.

The abundance of single males among the white collar workers was a boon to Cornwall's social life, leading to many a romance. In fact, a number of local girls married aqueduct employees, the most notable being the millionairess, Antoinette Gazzam, whose wedding to engineer Charles Galvin was an occasion of ostentatious extravagance. The policemen's ball in Matthiessen Hall was a popular event; and the police and other workers formed baseball teams which challenged the local players. A weekly column, "Along the Aqueduct Line", reported the games as well as personal items pertaining to the workers.

Another column recorded a less savory aspect of the aqueduct presence—crime. Although *The Local* treated the criminal activities among the construction crews with a light touch, there were plenty of fights, hold-ups, gambling, occasionally a murder. And if the number of arrests is any indication, there seemed to be plenty of hard liquor available, even though Cornwall was a "dry" town. A cocaine dealer was arrested, but drugs do not seem to have been a major problem.

Employment, housing, schools, recreation, and crime —in all these areas, Cornwall felt the impact of the aqueduct. If this were not enough, what about the dynamite explosion of 1911? It shattered windows, damaged buildings, inflicted injuries, and was felt as far away as Newburgh!

October 9, 1991

The Catskill Aqueduct, II

This "Stupendous Undertaking," as the Catskill Aqueduct was called, was the topic of an article in the *Van Norden Magazine* of January, 1907, an article which the Cornwall newspaper printed in its entirety. It contained a number of impressive statistics: the new water system for the City of New York would drain an area larger than Rhode Island; the dam to be constructed at Ashokan, second in size only to the Aswan Dam on the Nile River, would create a 12-mile-long reservoir that would engulf several towns; from there, an aqueduct seven feet in diameter would bring the water one hundred miles to New York. As an engineering feat, the project was compared to the Panama Canal.

New York City, growing at a rate of 125,000 per year, was in desperate straits for an expanded water supply. In 1905 a new Board of Water Supply had been established, with a mandate to explore all possible sources. After selecting the Catskill Plan as the most feasible, the Board hired five hundred engineers to make surveys and test borings to determine the best route. The plan was approved, at an estimated cost of 162 million dollars, to be financed by the issue of Water Supply bonds at 4%.

By 1907 work was underway in and around Cornwall. Several sites had been inspected and rejected for the river crossing; even a bridge had been considered. The final selection—a tunnel between Storm King and Breakneck Mountains—brought problems when the engineers realized that "all knowledge ... about the bed of the Hudson is inaccurate." When work stopped for the winter, the workers had not reached solid rock although they had drilled down seven hundred feet.

The construction firm of Mason and Hanger of Richmond, Kentucky, received the contract for the Cornwall sector at a cost of $3,492,800. The preliminaries took some time: erecting housing and other structures, including compressor plants and derrick towers at the shaft sites; and a new road led from the end of Bay View Avenue to shafts 7 and 8 at the base of Storm King Mountain. Soon work began in earnest. As each shaft was sunk

to the proper depth (between 300 and 500 feet), hoists were installed and horizontal tunnels, called headings, started in each direction. Mules were used to haul small cars along narrow gauge rails, bringing the debris to be hoisted to the surface. The compressor plants supplied the tunnel with ventilation and pneumatic power.

It was hazardous work. Many accidents were recorded and several fatalities. An ever-present menace was "popping rock" —the sudden fall of a piece of rock from an apparently smooth, solid surface; even a small fragment, dropping from a height, could be dangerous.

By 1911 the aqueduct project was half finished. A crew of three thousand worked at Ashokan, living in its own settlement of houses, stores, a bank, and a school which held evening classes in English and citizenship for the immigrant workers. A total work force of 16,000 was then under employment. That year work started on the tunnel under the Hudson River; bedrock had finally been reached and entrance shafts sunk to a depth of 1,200 feet. *The Local-Press* of February 1, 1912 featured the "holing through" ceremony. A party of officials from New York City, headed by Mayor Gaynor, was conveyed by elevator down to the tunnel. Here, the mayor pressed a button setting off a charge of dynamite which cleared away the last remaining section of rock. Afterwards, there were complimentary speeches followed by a banquet above ground. The Hudson tunnel, 3,000 feet long, was part of the 5.5-mile Moodna-Hudson-Breakneck siphon—into which the water would flow, then rise on the east side of the river to continue its course to the Kensico and Hill View Reservoirs. In recognition of this feature of the aqueduct, a poem "The Siphon Crew" appeared in *The Saturday Evening Post.*

In the spring, stone crushers at the shaft sites, also cement sheds, concrete mixers and belt conveyors signaled the final phase of the project—concreting the ceiling and sides of the tunnel. By working round the clock, the job was finished that fall and the closing of the shafts began. During 1913 the Hudson tunnel was being tested and the Ashokan Dam was nearing completion.

But it was 1916 before the aqueduct was finally in use. A weakness had developed in the tunnel near shaft 7, and a new construction team arrived to build another tunnel at this site; a test filling in 1915 showed that all was well. Then the Catskill water began to flow—600 million gallons per day—plunging into the siphon at Vails Gate, rushing under Cornwall and beneath the Hudson River to

rise of its own force and continue the three-day journey to New York.

Parallel to Drury Lane in New Windsor, you can see a large turf-covered mound; this is the aqueduct, at ground level here. At the foot of Breakneck Mountain, you can see a stone structure which marks the east end of the tunnel. These are the only visible indications of the vast subterranean tunnel beneath our town—the Catskill Aqueduct.

October 16, 1991

July 4, 1915

To the generations of Cornwall residents who have grown up with a Fourth of July Celebration, the program of 1915 will seem very familiar. Before that time, the observance of Independence Day had followed no set pattern. Firecrackers and sparklers, bought with long-hoarded savings, provided the children with a means of venting their patriotism. Some years there were athletic events—such as those held at the race track on Beakes Road in 1897, sponsored by the Red Men's Association. Or some of the summer residents would invite the public to fireworks displays on their estates. Firthcliffe residents could see the fireworks at Mr. Abell's.

The celebration of 1915 was a departure from these heretofore informal occasions. It was the brainchild of two village merchants, Samuel Van Tassell (whose men's clothing store occupied the large building across from the modern post office on Hudson Street) and William J. Lorch, a village trustee who had a poolroom nearby. An announcement of their intention appeared in the *Cornwall-Press* of June 3rd: "Samuel Van Tassell and William J. Lorch are on the committee to arrange for a Fourth of July celebration in Cornwall. There is no reason why this place cannot get up a rattling good celebration, and undoubtedly their project will be well received."

More details were soon forthcoming: the event was to be held at the playground (in the rear of the present Cornwall-on-Hudson Elementary School) and would consist of music, sports and fireworks. Harry W. Langworthy, school principal, agreed to be the treasurer,

and contributions were solicited from the public. One can imagine the co-chairmen popping in and out of each other's business places to consult about problems or to check the latest contributions. As the scope of the program became apparent, donations poured in and were listed in the newspaper. These made up in quantity what they lacked in amount; three people gave twenty-five dollars, several more five dollars, but one dollar was the usual donation.

"According to indications next Monday will be one of the biggest days Cornwall has ever had," boasted the *Cornwall-Press*. The program was set for July 5th as the Fourth fell on a Sunday. A description of all twenty-seven of the fireworks pieces was printed and the readers advised to save the list for reference on the great day.

The issue of July 8th carried a full account of the festivities. "Celebration Proves A Complete Success ... Remarkable Display of Fireworks The Feature, Committees Deserve Hearty Commendation For Excellent Work." The article started with the concern caused by "protracted and heavy rain in the fore part of the day"—a concern shared by many a future chairman — but the weather cleared by noon and the events began at two o'clock as scheduled, with Mr. Lorch as M.C.: invocation by Dr. W.W. Page of St. John's Church, and the address by Rev. Arthur N. Butz, pastor of the Cornwall Presbyterian Church, "who spoke eloquently of the tragedy now being enacted in the Old World, and the duties we owe to our country and to the men who made possible our present blessings;" next the reading of the Declaration of Independence by R.H. Barnett, a local attorney. Then the band struck up the National Anthem and a bomb was fired aloft, releasing an American flag.

Then came a baseball game between the two fire companies, Highland Engine, No. 1, defeating Storm King Engine, No.2. This was followed by a series of sports contests. Robert Quackenbush won the potato race, Frank Gould and Harry White the three-legged race, Wynne Toombs and A. Riddle the tandem race.

And there was more to come. The evening program opened with a concert by the Firthcliffe Band—when Mr. Van Tassell offered to make new uniforms for the group the preceding winter, did he have the Fourth of July in mind? Then came the climax, the fireworks, which were greeted with "plentiful applause." The spectators who had studied the published list were familiar with the pieces: the Grand

Illumination of the Grounds, the Electric Spiders, Niagara Falls, Flying Eagles, and Green-Eyed Monsters, to the Grand Finale —a display "of wide variety and exceptionally choice selection."

Afterwards, the indefatigable celebrants trooped off to Matthiessen Hall for dancing to the music of Frank Mead, "who always gives the kind of melodies that please."

Besides the general committee already mentioned, there was a committee on automobiles to handle parking—Fred Lorch and William J. Maroney; and a field committee of John Satterly and J.J. Lorch. The police on duty were George Toombs and James Watkins.

All together, Messrs. Van Tassell and Lorch had produced "a rattling good celebration"—a forerunner of Cornwall's modern Fourth of July.

July 3, 1991

The Graduation of 1916

Seventy-five years ago, nine seniors graduated from C.H.H.S., the Cornwall-on-Hudson High School, in a round of elaborate, tradition-filled events. In those days, the lower grades were very large by modern standards, but by the time the pupils reached high school, a considerable number had dropped out for one reason or another. The senior class might represent only a quarter of those who had entered the first grade twelve years before. No wonder the high school graduations were such elaborate occasions.

The festivities of 1916 opened on a Saturday night in June with the juniors' reception to the seniors, a dance attended by one hundred and thirty parents and friends. The school on Idlewild Avenue had no facilities for large gatherings, so Matthiessen Hall was the scene of all the functions. No one seemed to mind climbing the two long flights of stairs to the assembly hall on the top floor.

On Sunday evening, Rev. Butz of the Cornwall Presbyterian Church preached the baccalaureate. A resumé of his sermon con-

cluded with the ringing exhortation: "And now I bid you God-speed. You are stepping from the quiet and peace of the schoolroom into the noisome turbulent struggle of life." And he quoted from a lilting poem by Kipling.

The villagers again crowded into Matthiessen Hall on Tuesday night for the graduation exercises. Over the front of the stage was the class motto: "To Thine Own Self Be True" —in gold letters on a green background. These were the class colors, the class flower a rose.

The program began with an orchestral number and the invocation. Then the traditional essays—Marion F. Talbot read a paper, "Our Natural Resources," in which she optimistically stated that "We might be independent of all the countries at war, as soon as we find a substitute for a few chemicals and dyestuffs, which had been previously imported from Europe." World War I was then raging abroad.

After a vocal solo came the next essay: "An Imaginary Dinner" by Alice Slater, who "read with composure and in good voice an account of the various articles which go to make up a meal and their source." A piano solo preceded the honor oration by Robert C. Barnett which was entitled "Industrial Arbitration." It was noted that the boys had to memorize their offerings while the girls (the weaker sex?) were permitted to read theirs. Young Barnett wrestled manfully with "the history of capital and labor contentions" beginning with ancient Egypt. Pointing out the devastating effects of the 37,000 strikes in the United States in the past thirty-five years, he advocated the adoption of "compulsory arbitration" such as was being practiced in Australia.

Another vocal solo followed, after which Principal Harry W. Langworthy addressed the class of nine, paraphrasing Polonius' advice to Laertes in Hamlet: "to thine own better self be true," and urging each to "do his part to make the world a better place to live."

Mr. Adam B. Jaeger, president of the Board of Education, then came forward. He

"... expressed in felicitous words, the gratification and pride felt by the Board and the community in the achievements of the young people before him," and went on to award diplomas to Robert C. Barnett, Marion K. Chatfield, Agnes B. Deans, James A. Fredrickson, Frances G. O'Neill, Alice M. Slater, Carolyn L. Stevenson, Frank R. Talbot and Marion F. Talbot.

Mr. Jaeger's next duty was in the nature of a surprise—the presentation of a desk to Principal Langworthy who was leaving after nine years at the school—a token from the students and faculty.

Then, "Mr. Jaeger announced that chairs would be cleared from the center of the floor and dancing would be indulged in by those who wished, while an old-fashioned social visit would be enjoyed by all." The orchestra struck up the strains of a popular march and it was realized that the Commencement of Nineteen Sixteen would soon become a memory.

June 19, 1991

The World War - 1917

On April 6, 1917 America entered World War I. It is of interest to follow the impact of this momentous step in the pages of the local newspaper. The usual winter activities had taken place, but the war in Europe cast a shadow over this normalcy. Comments from leading citizens on the "present crisis" elicited the general consensus that war might still be avoided, but if it came, Americans could be counted on to do their duty. The Cornwall Relief Association met regularly to make garments and collect needed items for shipment abroad. Mrs. Pauline Sands Lee was in Paris, working with the American Aid for French Wounded; her letters often appeared in the paper. Other letters were from French soldiers thanking the townspeople for their generosity. Frank Velten, telegraph operator on a transatlantic liner, arrived home to tell of a perilous crossing from England. Miss Frances Hoppin pledged to care for sixty Belgian children for a year; her brother was in France, working for

the Red Cross. Banker James Stillman contributed $200,000 for the children of recipients of the French Legion of Honor.

Cornwall took on a martial character when a National Guard unit arrived to patrol the new aqueduct. After America's entry into the War, preparedness became the watchword. The Cornwall Rifle Club started military drill practice, directed by Adam B. Jaeger, a veteran of the Spanish-American War; they later formed the nucleus of a Home Guard. Food prices escalated and housewives were conscious of food shortages. The Equal Suffrage Club volunteered to match those having idle land with those willing to plant crops, especially potatoes; people even plowed up their front lawns to plant this staple.

After a few weeks, Cornwall men began to enlist. N.Y.M.A., the local recruiting station for officer training camp, received a number of applicants. Patriotic fervor quickened with the celebration of France Day on

April 26th. Marshal Joffre came to Newburgh for a gigantic parade and ceremonies at Washington's Headquarters, at which he appealed for American help in rebuilding France's railroad system. On Enrollment Day in June, over three hundred and fifty Cornwall males between the ages of twenty-one and thirty registered in their respective election districts. Meanwhile, enlistments continued. William Applebye-Robinson, formerly of the British navy, set a good example in this respect. After

obtaining his American citizenship, Robinson applied for enlistment in the U.S. Navy. On June 14th he received a commission in the naval reserve, and the following month was detailed to the *USS California*.

The town's Liberty Bond quota was $59,000. With the assistance of patriotic appeals in the paper and a Liberty Loan parade, Cornwall exceeded its quota by almost five thousand dollars.

April 15, 1992

The World War - 1918

The front door of the George J. Horobin house on Duncan Avenue carried a handsome bronze doorplate bearing an engraved inscription beneath the U.S. seal: "This house has given two men to the service defending the cause of God, Humanity and America" —a sentiment to which the majority of Cornwall would have subscribed. Two Horobin sons were in service—Walter and Pryor.

It was October, 1918; no one realized how soon the war would be over, although the news from abroad was encouraging. Cornwall had contributed generously to the Fourth Liberty Loan and was prepared to aid the United War Work Campaign which was about to launch a drive. The Honor Roll, appearing each week in the *Cornwall Press*, contained the names of over three hundred and fifty men and women in the armed forces; each month brought additions to the list and sometimes to the number of fatalities and wounded. It was a great occasion for families when their sons came home on furlough; they saw to it that such visits were given coverage in the newspaper along with any promotions in rank. Families were also proud to share the correspondence of their servicemen—these homey, frank letters give a graphic picture of personal experiences.

"Dear Mother,
Well, Ma, we have just come back from our second front and we are now resting up after making a pretty creditable showing .... Up until now it has not been bad

soldiering over here; however thoughts of the oncoming winter are not very pleasant and I would just as soon spend it at home ....
"Well, Ma, I received the letter with the little prayer in it and I am memorizing it ... I do not get the chance to go to Mass as often over here as I did back home, but I go in a different and better way over here."
Cpl. Edwin L. Gibbons

"Dear Mother:
A few lines to tell you I am alive. I am in the dugout.... It is a place in the ground dug out long ago, packed with logs and sandbags and made shellproof. Inside there are two tiers of bunks, perhaps 4 or 6 bunks in the place. There is a wide aisle and plenty of room to get around. In case a shell comes over you must run for the dugout as it is the only safe place."
Pvt. William Kane

From Melvin Campbell to William B. Cocks (he had worked at Cocks Store):

We "... have been very busy on the Cambrai - St. Quentin front ... and worst of all I had to be the first one to be picked off [he was hit by a machine gun bullet] .... Well after the doctor bandaged my leg I started on and caught up with the battalion Headquarters in time to be in another skirmish ... We charged in on them ... took 40 prisoners." After which, Campbell hobbled back two miles to the advance dressing station and was sent to the hospital at Havre from where he was writing.

From George Birdsall, Jr. to Mr. A.C. Case:

"The work I am doing now is quite hard... I have seen quite a lot of France as I have been doing convoy work... We are all hoping against hope that we will be home for Christmas 1918..."

From Pvt. William J. Dwyer:

"We are busy all the time and we do not get much time for pleasure, still we have no kick coming....[As for the war] It is all ready won. I like France a little.... All you need in this life is health and a little nerve .... Since I left [nearly three years ago] I have had quite a little experience ... but Cornwall is the only place worth while remembering."

From Tom Donahue:

"Well we are still going, facing the enemy and expect big things before long .... By the tone of the prisoners ... they begin to see their failure. I don't blame them. I would not care to face such artillery and troops as we have myself..."

Back at home, the fall activities were beginning. The Firthcliffe ladies started a bowling league, but also put in long hours at the Red Cross headquarters in the Firthcliffe engine house. The Epworth League of the Methodist Church sponsored a series of debates on timely topics—the war and woman suffrage. Hunters were getting licenses in anticipation of the hunting season, promising to bring home a large deer from the Catskills or Adirondacks. Although their annual clambake had been cancelled, the Mountainville Grange was holding regular meetings. The women's weekly card parties and sewing groups had been superseded by Red Cross work; a report for the year contained incredible statistics: 508 hospital garments made and 1,784 knitted items, 86 boys outfitted with sweaters and socks, and a total of 79,237 surgical dressings made! A Home Service Department was proving very useful in keeping soldiers in touch with their families and rendering aid to their dependents.

The Newburgh Shipyards, where twelve 9,000-ton cargo steamers were under construction, advertised for two thousand workers to join the three thousand already employed there. Carpenters and masons were also needed to build two hundred houses. So many Cornwall men worked at the shipyards that a special bus transported them to and from work.

Then came the terrible influenza epidemic which struck the Atlantic seaboard some time in September, apparently from Europe where it had been raging. It lasted for only a few months, but, during that time, hardly a Cornwall family was left untouched, especially adults between twenty and forty. First the schools closed, then the churches; for a time all public gatherings were banned.

The George Mailler family in Cliffside Park lost two daughters, Margaret and Enid. Cornwall undertaker, Edward L. Sylcox, ran out of coffins and had to commission a local carpenter to make them. Sometimes an entire family was stricken. To alleviate these emergencies, the Red Cross stepped in—Dr. Morton Peck and Mrs. Hawthorne, a retired nurse, assisted by other members. "The squad has been of invaluable service in cases where whole families have been confined to bed." The Cornwall Canteen workers—in anticipation of the future Meals on Wheels—distributed broth, jellies and other nourishing food.

Little was known either of the cause or treatment of the epidemic, but the local health officer issued sensible preventive measures and dispelled the widely-held notion that wearing camphor would make one immune. The State Health Department also warned of debilitating aftereffects.

Then, as quickly as it had come, the epidemic passed, and Cornwall could rejoice with the rest of the nation in the Armistice.

November 4, 1992

On the Homefront

The fall of 1918 was an historic time when Cornwall, with the rest of the nation, felt the effect of critical events abroad. Even though decisive actions on the European front filled the newspapers, people did not realize how soon the fighting would be over.

The war continued to permeate the fabric of daily life. On September 5th, all males between 18 and 45 were required to register if they had not already done so. Several of the local lawyers volunteered to help the registrants in filling out the questionnaires for a draft that was later to be cancelled.

Large posters in the newspapers announced the 4th Liberty Loan with the slogan: "Build Tanks to Break the Hindenburg Line." A Liberty Loan Train, filled with an exhibit of war trophies, stopped at Cornwall Landing the evening of September 26th. The Cornwall Home Guard was on hand, also the Boy Scouts, who outdid themselves by securing twenty-two Liberty Loan subscriptions from visitors to the exhibit.

While Cornwall boys were serving overseas or at U.S. posts, while those beyond the age for service or otherwise disqualified were employed in essential industries or enrolled in the Home Guard, the women of Cornwall did their bit—in fact they were indefatigable. These efforts were channeled through the Red Cross, the War Relief Association and the Canteen. Children were also expected to help in the war effort: the Boy Scouts and the Junior Red Cross, who made scrapbooks for veterans' hospitals. That fall there was a new demand — with horrible implications — the collection of fruit pits and the shells of certain nuts to be used in making charcoal, "the most effective material for neutralizing poison gas in gas masks." Receptacles were placed around town for the deposit of these items.

Regulations were still in force. Housewives had to apply for a sugar card to obtain enough sugar for the fall canning. They had to stretch the family food budget to include the rise in prices—milk was now 13¢ a quart and butter was selling at 69¢ a pound. Village and town officials were negotiating with government fuel commissioners to expedite Cornwall's allotment of coal. The public was urged to save this scarce commodity by burning wood.

One of the most exciting incidents of the fall was provided by Colonel Milton F. Davis, then commandant at N.Y.M.A., who was on leave as chief of training of the U.S. Air Service. Having official business in the area, Colonel Davis flew from Washington, D.C. in a De Haviland warplane, piloted by his assistant, and landed on the N.Y.M.A. parade ground. "The word had been passed around in Cornwall of the prospective aerial visitors and everyone was on the lookout for a glimpse of them." On approaching, the plane circled several times over the town, flying "quite low." The landing was marred slightly when "the machine nosed into an unseen mound of earth at the boundary of the old tennis court," causing slight damage to the propellor blades and radiator. Repairs delayed the departure for a day, during which time a guard was detailed to watch over the plane.

The newspaper article stated that Colonel Davis had been receiving daily instruction in flying—the oldest man in the service to do so. Despite this and other sterling abilities, it was his flying a warplane to Cornwall that made him the hero of the day. How many young boys dreamed of a future career in aviation as the result of "Cornwall's First Aerial Visitor" and how many extra Liberty Bonds were purchased by their elders after they had seen at first hand what their dollars had already accomplished?

October 28, 1992

Women's War Work

Although the 19th Amendment giving nationwide suffrage to women would not be ratified until 1920, the movement was gaining strength during World War I, and was no doubt responsible for expanding the role of women in the war effort.

During 1917-18 the *Cornwall Press* published an Honor Roll, listing the local men and women in the various branches of the Armed Forces. By 1918 the names of six Cornwall girls could be found there: Misses Grace Davis, Mary K. Furey, Alida Garrison, Anna P. Nolan, Justine C. Todd and Jennie S. Vail. All were serving as nurses—abroad or at soldiers hospitals in the United States. Two Cornwall women held civilian positions in Europe: Miss Frances Hoppin, a Red Cross worker, and the redoubtable Mrs. Lee, who was serving as a representative of the American Fund for French Wounded. A number of local girls also had government jobs in Washington, D.C. or were replacing male telegraph operators at various locations.

There was ample need for women volunteers on the homefront. The Red Cross authorized a chapter in Cornwall with headquarters on Main Street and auxiliary workrooms in other parts of the town: on the second floor of the Village Office, in the fire house on Willow Avenue, in Mountainville and on the mountain. All of these Stations were needed to meet the monthly quota of 10,000 dressings, the clothing to be made and collected, the articles to be knitted. And to raise funds for materials, the women organized a constant round of dances, musicals, teas and food sales—whose proceeds supplemented the regular Red Cross Drive.

The Old Homestead was another center for war-related projects. Cornwall had close ties with France, primarily through Mrs. Lee and some of the mountain residents. The old house became the headquarters of the Cornwall War Relief Association, an affiliation of the American Fund for French Wounded. Working with the Newburgh branch, this group raised substantial funds, part of which went toward an ambulance, and they collected and shipped abroad an incredible quantity of foodstuffs and clothing. Mrs. William Apple-

bye-Robinson and her committee spearheaded these efforts. Another project was Christmas bags to be sent to soldiers in French hospitals—the goal for 1918 was one thousand. These bags contained such useful items as writing tablet, envelopes and pencils; a pipe and tobacco pouch; sewing kit, razor, soap, handkerchiefs, gum and candy.

The Old Homestead Tea Room—open from May till November—donated the entire proceeds of its 1918 season to the War Relief Association; and the profits from the annual fair were divided among the local war relief organizations.

Another group of women, the Cornwall Canteen, had as its aim the morale of new soldiers enroute to military service. They joined with the Newburgh Canteen to form squads which met the troop trains halting at Cornwall Landing to refuel. The volunteers wore a blue apron with white collars and cuffs, and a blue cap trimmed with white. A white band on the left arm bore the label "Canteen." The project was such a success that Miss Mary Young, the purchasing agent, had to keep a large stock of supplies on hand. The workers solicited contributions from townspeople and from the passengers of the boats and trains stopping at the Landing. The *Cornwall Press* frequently printed letters the Canteen workers had received, adding: "The boys appreciate the service... as is demonstrated when they leave and give three hearty cheers for Cornwall and the Cornwall Canteen."

A story on the Canteen appeared one Sunday in the *New York Herald*. "For the past two months the canteen has been supplying refreshments daily for an average of 1,500 men, though there have been single days when as many as 10,000 were served. When word is received that a troop train is coming the young women rush ... [to the Landing] where they supply the men with hot or iced tea or coffee, cigarettes, chocolate and chewing gum." They were often called to dispense post cards and stamps, to mail or even write a letter, to provide "comfort bags" and even minor first aid!

The farmerettes were another type of volunteer. A group of girls from New York City was joined by three Cornwall girls. They were paid twenty-five cents an hour for farm or garden work, two dollars for an eight-hour day. With the shortage of male labor, the girls provided a needed service.

It is interesting to note that men occupied the top positions in some of these organizations. However, Mrs. Lee had founded the War Relief Association and Mrs. Robinson was its president in 1918. And it was the women who helped raise the money, who made the bandages, knitted and sewed; who collected and packed the overseas shipments; who met the troop trains. In two years they would have the vote.

November 18, 1992

Armistice Day, 1918

Armistice Day in Cornwall, November 11, 1918, was a 24-hour nonstop gala, the like of which had not been experienced before. In fact there were two celebrations. Premature, impromptu bursts of jollification erupted on November 7th, when word was received of Germany's surrender. The village fire siren blew at 2 P.M.,— the signal for church bells and whistles to join in. The two fire companies hastily trimmed their apparatus and drove around town making as much noise as possible. The schools were dismissed; some of the village children decorated the old Storm King Engine hose cart; the boys hauled it through the village filled with girls waving American flags. That evening a "rattling good parade manifested the joy of the town."

The townspeople's spirits were in no way dampened by this anticlimax. They had the weekend to co-ordinate plans for the bona fide celebration on Monday, the 11th, when it was confirmed that the armistice had been signed.

The *Cornwall Press* devoted several columns to an account of the day. "The coal dock whistle was the first, we believe, to announce the wonderful news. Mead and Taft Company's whistle and the fire siren took up the glad refrain. The bells of the village were a little slow in getting started, but pretty soon Village Clerk F.B. King appeared with the key and got the Presbyterian church bell busy. About this time, the Liberty Bell at the Fire House came in on the chorus." The newspaper office was located on Hudson Street next to the church; the staff must have been immersed all day in a cacophony of bells!

It did not take long for the coal dock workers on Shore Road to get up a parade. About fifty of them came marching up River Avenue, then along Hudson Street, down Dock Hill and back to the point of departure. "Each man was holding onto a long rope, which passed the length of the procession and at the rear was attached to a dummy Kaiser, who was being ignominiously drawn through the streets."

After lunch, crowds flocked to Newburgh to witness the gigantic parade there. Units from Cornwall participated: the women of the War Relief Association and motor apparatus from the fire companies.

Cornwall's parade came that evening. Fred Booth, Firth Carpet Company superintendent, was chairman, with Morris M. Davidson of the Home Defense Corps and John S. Holloran as marshals. The N.Y.M.A. band and corps of cadets led the parade "in splendid martial formation," followed by town, village and school officials. The Cornwall branch of the Red Cross was preceded by young Lee B. Mailler,[1] "artistically draped in Red Cross costume and volubly blowing a horn." Then came the Cornwall Home Defense Corps, the War Relief Association (marching in its second parade of the day), the Boy Scouts, Canteen workers and the Knights of Pythias. The school children paraded, also Braden's School and the Village Band. Bringing up the rear

---

1 Mailler (1898-1967) was later superintendent of the Cornwall Hospital and a Majority Leader of the New York State Assembly.

were the local fire companies and a bevy of decorated bicycles.

After the regular parade had disbanded, a group of two hundred celebrators, led by a bass drum and two fifes, marched back and forth along Main Street, giving vent to their joy by means of dinner bells, horns and tin pans. It was nearly midnight when they finally dispersed after burning several effigies of the Kaiser in one huge blaze. But Storm King Engine's "Liberty Bell" kept tolling sporadically into the night. School children had taken turns ringing it during the day; after dark some pranksters attached a long rope to the bell, the end of which led behind the fire house. From this secluded spot, they were able "to ring the bell at will."

Thanksgiving came that year on November 28th. President Wilson's proclamation read in part: "It has long been our custom to turn in the autumn of the year in praise and thanksgiving to Almighty God for His many blessings and mercies to us as a Nation. This year we have special and moving cause to be grateful and to rejoice." If the tone of Armistice Day had been one of exuberant jubilation, that of Thanksgiving was more somber. The Methodist Church held a Harvest Home Service, at which time the public was asked to contribute food and clothing for the needy, especially those families who had suffered from the influenza epidemic.

And a *Cornwall Press* editorial reflected the mood in more than one Cornwall home: "Thanksgiving Day this year cannot be observed with the old-time abandon and happiness, though there is tremendous cause for devout thanksgiving... But in many homes throughout the country there are vacant chairs, holding memories that can never be effaced." The war had left many scars.

November 11, 1992

Memorial Day, 1920

Cornwall's Memorial Day of 1920 was a unique occasion in the annals of town history—is there anyone who remembers that memorable day? Another question: how many times a week do you pass the Soldiers' Monument near the Town Hall? Is your attention so focused on making the green light that, like most passersby, you are scarcely aware of the granite shaft and accompanying cannon on the small plot between two busy roads? The monument and older cannon are memorials to veterans of the Civil War; the second cannon, from World War I, was presented to the town on Memorial Day, 1920.

The event was fully covered by the *Cornwall Press*, beginning with a special edition on May 27th, its cover printed on glossy paper bordered by a red and blue stripe, the masthead flanked by American and French flags. The headline "Significant Event Staged for Memorial Day in Cornwall" was followed by the details: "Captain Pierre Lecomte du Nouy, a distinguished citizen of France — an embattled soldier of the Great World War — representing the French Government will present to the people of Cornwall, in the name of his country, a seventy-seven milimetre cannon, captured from the Germans in combat." Taken "when the German army made its final fatal drive against Paris...it is the only captured cannon of the great World War ever presented to an American community." This great honor, the article continued, was due to the efforts of Dr. Ernest G. Stillman.

Column one of the newspaper lists the parade's line of march. Forming at the Village Square, it would proceed down Hudson Street as far as Mountain Road, countermarch to the upper village and onto Willow Avenue to the Firthcliffe Club, then return to the Monument where the ceremonies would take place. Spectators lining the parade route would see an impressive number of units. The first division, headed by the N.Y.M.A. Band, consisted of veterans of the Civil War, the Spanish-American and World Wars, the corps of cadets, and what everyone would crane his neck to see, Captain du Nouy on horseback escorting the horse-drawn cannon. The Firthcliffe Band provided music for the second division, which included town and village dignitaries, thirteen civic and fraternal organizations, and students from the public and parochial schools and Storm King School. At the end of the parade were the Storm King and Highland Engine Companies and the Cornwall Village Band.

On page two of the paper was listed "The Veteran Dead of Cornwall," a total of one hundred and seven, buried in ten town and neighboring cemeteries.

The editor's prediction that Cornwall would welcome the Frenchman with open arms was borne out by the June 3rd issue, which featured the presentation ceremony and printed the text of Captain du Nouy's speech. "I am no speechmaker," he began, "and I hate nothing so much as speaking in public. But today is different.... This gun is yours, and has been chosen for you by myself, three thousand miles away, at the muddy camp where it was brought right after it had been captured near Soissons....

"I love this country," he continued, "because of its high ideals, backed by the most wonderful energy, and the most striking boldness." He spoke of his homeland—its wartorn devastation, from which it was "coming back to life in the most astonishing way," and the great gratitude it felt for America.

The editor was eloquent in praise. "As an ambassador of peace he [du Nouy] fulfilled a beautiful mission; as an educator he enhanced our learning; as a gentleman he taught us a lesson and gave himself as an example."

Supervisor Clemence C. Smith, in accepting the German cannon on behalf of the town, read an original poem he had written for the occasion. Then Mrs. Cyrus W. Shaw read the Gettysburg Address, also "a verse in appreciation of the boys of the World War." Commented the editor: "Mrs. Shaw has an excellent voice and a clear delivery." The address of Dr. Jay W. Somerville, "an old-time orator," was clearly superfluous, and received scant coverage.

At the conclusion of the ceremony, the Old Homestead lawn was the scene of an informal reception, a time for the townspeople to meet Captain du Nouy in person. This part of the program inspired another burst of eloquence from the editor on the impression made by the Frenchman. "He sank his own personality in the higher motive of the celebration and joined heartily with the people of Cornwall in the inspiring sentiments of the day, met them like a brother, caressed the children, honored the old warriors, praised the valor of their courageous youth, and charmed the whole town by the comradeship of his gentle nature. The children loved him at once. They followed his horse in the parade and gazed at the man in an admiring wonder."

At midday, the official party of thirty retired to Red Men's Hall for a sumptuous luncheon at which Dr. Stillman was the toastmaster. A picture of the group in front of the building is preserved in the town archives. Captain du Nouy appears in the center flanked by the surviving veterans of the Civil War. Also in the picture are Colonel Milton F. Davis, superintendent of N.Y.M.A., the town and village boards, a delegation from the American Legion, and Dr. Stillman.

Another memento of the event is a film, probably taken by Dr. Stillman—now so fragile that it breaks repeatedly when shown. But what a unique document! It shows Captain du Nouy on horseback surrounded by a group of children, the war veterans marching by and scenes at the Monument. It is interesting to note the rural character of the town in 1920.

The next time you drive past the Monument Park, think about the Memorial Day of 1920.

May 25, 1994

A Community Christmas Tree

A Christmas tree from the 1920s engenders a variety of thoughts on Cornwall's past.

Early in that decade, the *Cornwall Press* started to publish a special Christmas edition of eighteen pages, twice the size of the usual paper. The editor must have worked diligently to fill this expanded issue. He invited the Cornwall clergy to submit Christmas messages, also the principals from the two high schools. He sponsored a Christmas story contest and published the prize-winning effort. The issue also contained details of the many Christmas events in the schools, churches, fraternal and other organizations—for a town whose population was much smaller than at present, there was a remarkable number of seasonal activities. The churches held Christmas services, enriched by special musical offerings, and the Sunday Schools of each denomination staged elaborate entertainments, climaxed by the appearance of a rotund Santa with a gift-filled sack. A youngster from Firthcliffe could easily be involved in three different events: at school and Sunday School, and in the annual party sponsored by the Firth Carpet Company at the Firthcliffe Club. The remainder of the issue contained ads, ranging from a full page by the Cornwall National Bank to smaller, less expensive ads listing the Christmas wares of local and Newburgh merchants. A picture in full color adorned the entire front page.

This pretentious edition was part of a crusade spearheaded by the *Cornwall Press* and the Chamber of Commerce to create a "Greater Cornwall"—to boost the town's image in the aftermath of the post- war depression. A vote to enlarge the incorporated village of Cornwall by encompassing other sections of the town was held up in courts for several years until it was finally defeated. The opening of the Storm King Highway was viewed as a precursor of a new age of prosperity. A few inns, tourist homes and gas stations did open, but the traffic problem was not solved until the construction of the 9W Bypass over the mountains in 1940. Dr. Ernest G. Stillman had founded the Cornwall Industrial Corporation to provide jobs in a number of fields and there was talk of building a hospital.

Not the least among these new initiatives, at least symbolically, was a community Christmas tree, indicative of a new unity, which had been lacking in the rivalry between Cornwall's "upper" and "lower" villages. The site, appropriately, was the lawn of the Old Homestead (the Sands-Ring House) where stood "a great cedar which has braved the storms of many years and grown to a beautiful proportion..." Exclaimed the newspaper of December, 1921: "Cornwall will have a Community Christmas tree—the first in its history—advancing... the forward march of Greater Cornwall." The whole town was invited to participate in a short program on Christmas Eve, after which the Old Homestead would be open for refreshments. A chorus of seventy-five voices, composed of the united church choirs, would sing carols; there would be a prayer, a reading of the Christmas story, and a message from one of the town's most civic-minded citizens, General Milton F. Davis, N.Y.M.A. superintendent and Chamber of Commerce president. After the ceremony, the choir would sing at the homes of shut-ins. In praising this new Yuletide event, the editor could not resist pointing out how it would unite the community —"the main thing toward which all our civic energies are now happily devoted." And he added a sentimental note: if any firesides lacked a tree, the community tree "will fill the vacancy." In a lighter vein, he declared as false the rumor that the ladies of the Old Homestead planned to hang their stockings on the tree in hopes that a miracle would bring them husbands. He added, however, that a town clergyman had confided that if he had his way, he would provide every girl with "a perfectly eligible husband" and would be happy to perform the marriage service gratis!

Unfortunately, a storm postponed the Christmas Eve ceremony at the tree, but it took place the following night before a large audience. The decorated tree was the creation of two young electricians, Hand and Ohlson, who had covered it with a myriad of electric lights, and of Central Hudson, who had supplied the cable connection and current free of charge. To perpetuate this new community tradition, it was suggested that donations be made for the purchase of electrical equipment.

The Christmas ceremony at the Old Homestead cedar was held again in 1922, with Rev. John F. Hagen of the Cornwall Presbyterian Church presiding and General Davis again the speaker. The *Cornwall Press* commented enthusiastically:"Nothing which has happened in a generation has done so much to weld together the people of Cornwall as this magnificent tree and the Community singing." Another innovation was a request for residents to place a light in their front windows on Christmas Eve. Both traditions were to continue for several years.

The selection of the Old Homestead as the site for the community tree was a fitting one, in conformity with the prevailing spirit of unity. A joint effort by the two Village Improvement Societies had saved the historic house from demolition; and their unremitting labors brought about its renovation and use as a community center, a role which had started in the 18th century when the home of David Sands had been a meeting place for the Cornwall Quakers. During the Civil War and World War I, the house was headquarters for women's war relief efforts; for several years, dances were held in the pavilion on the grounds and for a time it was the quarters of the American Legion. Today it is the scene of a colonial crafts school program.

In addition to these activities—by virtue of its 230-year history and its proximity to the Town Hall Park—this historic old house remains a community center, even though there is no longer a cedar tree to unite the town at Christmas.

December 14, 1994

The Storm King Highway

"Convention Marks Actual Opening of Storm King Road"—this headline in the *Cornwall Press* of October 1922 takes note of another important event in Cornwall history.

From planning stage to completion, the Storm King Highway had been beset with difficulties—lack of funds, politics, engineering and construction hazards, work stoppages—but by 1922 the magnificent scenic highway was finally completed. Only one problem remained—when to hold the official opening. The State Highway Commissioner was adamant about postponing the date for another year until the route through Cornwall could be upgraded to handle the anticipated flow of traffic. But local politicians considered such a delay unreasonable. The village bandstand had already been moved from its position in the center of Hudson Street. Whether this street should be widened or traffic rerouted onto a new road was a squabble not likely to be resolved immediately. Why not open the highway at once?

Accordingly, a Celebration Committee began to formulate grandiose plans. A bill passed the state legislature authorizing Cornwall to raise five thousand dollars to cover the celebration expenses—a measure hotly opposed by local taxpayers when they realized they would be paying the extra levy. The *Cornwall Press* seems to have straddled the issue; at first it broached the possibility of a July Fourth opening, then suggested that Cornwall "go it alone" and ignore the dilatory Celebration Commission. A later editorial reversed this opinion by stating that the highway should not be opened until the Cornwall approach was completed—otherwise there would be "unbelievable congestion." While the opening date was under discussion, frequent attempts were made to traverse the highway. The first commercial truck passed over the road in February 1922. In April a guard had to be posted to prevent the "passage of determined motorists." But it was impossible to stem the tide of curious pedestrians—"Many Easter hikers on highway," reported the newspaper. And the public had to be warned against throwing objects over the side onto the railroad tracks below.

The local fire companies—Highland Engine, No.1 and Storm King Engine, No.

2—entered the picture by negotiating to have the annual County Firemen's Convention held in Cornwall in October 1922. This was no small undertaking, and the firemen spent months in preparation—soliciting donations, inviting area fire companies to participate, and attending to a myriad of other details. The *Cornwall Press* kept its readers informed as the plans progressed, listing the fire companies as word of their acceptance was received. In fact, the convention news supplanted all mention of the Celebration Commission. Beginning in July, a special masthead appeared on page one, showing six firemen pulling an old-fashioned fire engine on which was printed: "Orange County Volunteer Firemen's Convention, October 5, 1922." In anticipation of the event, the Cornwall firemen spared no efforts to make a good showing. Both companies were having new uniforms made; the brick facade of the Highland Engine fire house was being cleaned, the interior refurbished, and the brasswork of the Pierce-Arrow apparatus "nickeled."

As October drew near, the newspaper coverage escalated, with notes about the participants, the line of march and the schedule of events. In the September 21st issue came to the astonishing news: "Visiting Firemen are to have the Storm King Road opened to them."

On October 5th the *Cornwall Press* published a special edition in honor of the convention and the next week gave a full account of the affair. A morning meeting of the convention delegates at Red Men's Hall had been followed by a luncheon served by several of the local churches and organizations. Then came a parade of fire apparatus, a highly successful innovation which gave the fire companies an opportunity to view each other's equipment. The main parade set out at 3 P.M. — forty-six fire companies interspersed with bands and fife and drum corps. Beginning at the Main Street bandstand (the traffic circle), it proceeded along Main and Hudson Streets to Cornwall Landing, then countermarched to the upper village, ending at the Morgan Horse Farm, where a dinner was served in a huge marquee to two thousand people. Speeches, a movie on fire fighting equipment, fireworks and dancing brought the day to a close. And in between these events, the firemen had inspected the new highway.

Dr. Ernest G. Stillman, a keen firemanic enthusiast, had hosted a luncheon that day at his home on Mountain Road for some sixty state and local dignitaries, and it was there that history was made — with the announcement that the Storm King Highway was now officially open. One of the guests, John L. Hayes, contractor of the highway construction, confirmed the statement by saying: "Storm King Road is now definitely open and I have every reason to believe I shall see the fulfillment of my hope that it will always stay open." How would he have reacted to the frequent and prolonged closings over the past years?

October 20, 1993

The Dog Shows at Kenridge Farm

The purchase of the former Kenridge Farm by the Scenic Hudson Land Trust brings into prominence a choice tract of land which is filled with history. This property is located on the outskirts of Cornwall, bordered by Route 9W and Angola Road. Traditionally the site of an early 18th century settlement, it later became the home of Congressman Lewis Beach, Cornwall's first historian. In the 1890s, James Stillman acquired the farm as an addition to his Ridge Road estate, where he had recently built a summer home (now Jogue's Retreat). To quote from an old *Local*: "In the fertile valley at the base of historic Storm King Mountain, James [Stillman] established Kenridge Farm, stocked with registered Jersey cattle, which was considered the showplace of Cornwall." Here he built a mammoth barn which swallowed up a smaller structure; other outbuildings included a blacksmith shop, stables and houses for poultry. A manager occupied the farm house on the property.

It is James' son, Chauncey, (formally known as Charles Chauncey) who is more closely identified with Kenridge Farm in the 20th century. Before 1912 the early Cornwall newspapers recorded the milestones in Chauncey's life: college graduation, marriage, the birth of children, trips to the West on railroad business, and occasional visits to Cornwall. But after that date, he seems to have spent more time here, summering at the Ridge Road estate, and developing the farm in accordance with his hobbies.

An item from *The Local Press* of 1912 states: "On the former Van Ness farm at Cornwall there are gathered together a few well-bred Morgan mares. Come and see." On this property, adjoining Kenridge Farm, Chauncey bred and raised Morgan horses, which he exhibited each fall at the Vermont State Fair. A 1915 article from *The Local* carried the headline: "The Morgan Horse Farm at Cornwall, N.Y. — a Thriving New Industry." To Cornwall residents, the horses were a familiar sight for they were exercised on the public roads. And on view at the bank were some of the prizes they had won when exhibited at shows and fairs. "Oxen and Oratory at the Horse Farm" described an outing of the Orange County Farm Bureau in 1919 attended by six thousand people. The program included speeches, band concert, an exhibit of Stillman's horses, and an oxen roast— "a bully good time."

Chauncey Stillman died suddenly in August, 1926, while homeward bound from a European trip. An interest in dogs had led him to establish kennels on the west side of Ridge Road, and he had been active in the organization of the Storm King Kennel Club. His untimely death occurred as he was returning home for the club's second annual dog show.

The first show had been held on August 22, 1925 "at Kenridge Farm's Race Track"—on the site of the 19th-century track built by Lewis Beach. "Enter your pets," urged the club, "and have them passed upon by expert officials." The show was under the supervision of Frank Dole of the *New York Tribune* and "an expert judging list has been compiled." In addition to trophies and ribbons, $1,500 in cash prizes would be awarded.

The second show in 1926 was a more ambitious affair, which set the pattern for the next decade. Large tents were set up at the race track—one where the dogs were exhibited, another where the judging took place, another for the food concessions, usually handled by the American Legion. "Its natural scenic setting is superb," commented the local newspaper after the dog show had become an established event; "the quality of the entries is usually high, the management efficient, the judging competent and the whole atmosphere of the affair that of a real sporting event..." The location was ideal, with spacious grounds and ample room for parking. The exhibitors paid only three dollars for each dog entered, and they were guests of the club for lunch. There was no admission fee— "the only free show in the country," boasted the club.

Many old timers remember the dog shows, which were held in late summer. About a month before the event, notices would appear in the newspaper announcing the date, deadline for entries, prizes to be offered, and a list of the judges. Afterward came a write-up of the show: the number of dogs entered, the different breeds exhibited, and the prize winners—interspersed with superlatives; each year, it seemed, the dog show was bigger and better!

Over seven hundred dogs were entered in 1927 and the president's cup was won by a wire-haired terrier, shown for the first time in the United States. By now an entire column was required to list all the winners. It was customary for the Firthcliffe Band to perform during the afternoon, but in 1929, the concert took place prior to the judging, as the music tended to upset some of the dogs!

A children's class was added; in 1935 the 680 entries included thirty-seven different breeds. In 1936 the "notables" vied for attention with the canines: among those present were Jimmy Walker, ex-mayor of New York, and his wife, the former Betty Compton. Also present were Hamilton Fish, Jr., Bob Simmons, a popular radio star, and Bud Fisher, creator of the Mutt and Jeff comic strip. Although most of the entries were from out of town, there were a number of local winners:

Edward Krug, Mrs. Ralph E. Ogden, Mrs. Ingalls, and Rev. Thomas Prendergast of St. Thomas Church. Some years the weather was very bad, but it did not deter the crowds, and the tents provided some protection from the rain. The opening of the Bypass (Route 9W)

in 1940 seems to have put an end to the dog shows—the highway obliterated the old race track.

November 17, 1993
November 24, 1993

The Cornwall Hospital

It was sixty years ago this week, April 6, 1931, that The Cornwall Hospital opened its doors—a memorable occasion for a small town. It merited a banner headline in *The Cornwall Local:* "Huge Throng Attends Official Opening of Cornwall Hospital." The article went on to describe festivities, which began with a parade up Main Street and over to the hospital grounds. Led by the N.Y.M.A. Band, the American Legion Post and its Auxiliary proudly escorted a new ambulance—their gift to the hospital. It had taken several years to raise the money for this ambitious undertaking, with countless fund-raisers and appeals for contributions.

The assembled crowd on the hospital lawn must have cheered with enthusiasm as the parade approached; then they settled down for formal exercises, which included remarks by Andrew G. Mapes, president of the hospital Board of Managers, and by the donor, Dr. Ernest G. Stillman. In a short speech, Dr. Stillman related how the hospital came to be built—a story now part of Cornwall history. "Some years ago," he said, "I was asked to see a sick child. As the patient was in dire need of hospital care to save her life, I rushed her in my car to an adjacent hospital. But the hospital would not admit the patient and the child died. That tragedy marks the starting of the Cornwall Hospital. It seems almost as if that child died so that future generations of Cornwall children would have a hospital of their own. I am deeply grateful that I have been permitted to carry out this longfelt wish. The Cornwall Hospital is now a fact. The bricks have been laid and the furniture placed." The facility, equipped to the last detail with the

most modern technology for its day, was a gift to the community from Dr. Stillman and his wife.

"Following the exercises," continued *The Local*, "the guests were allowed to inspect the building and were held speechless at such a magnificent structure so splendidly equipped." [The crowd was so large that another open house was scheduled for the next day.] From the panelled reception room, the capacious kitchen and nurses' dining room, to the comfortable patient rooms and the departments: surgical, obstetrical, X-ray and laboratory, the total effect was one of efficiency and good taste."

It had taken almost a decade from the incorporation in 1923 to realize Dr. Stillman's dream. The first steps in the implementation of this facility came that year, when Dr. Stillman organized a group of residents for the purpose of applying to Albany for incorporation papers. Next, a Board of Managers was appointed and Dr. Stillman sold a block of lots in Highland View Park to help finance the enterprise. Another portion of this development sloping eastward with a magnificent view of the mountains was selected for the site of the new hospital.

After several years' planning, construction began in 1929 and the cornerstone was laid on Memorial Day, 1930. The usual parade, instead of disbanding at the Monument, proceeded to the hospital site for the laying of the cornerstone. *The Local* described the exercises and listed all of the forty-seven articles placed in the cornerstone. Eleven months later the building opened.

An early brochure described the impressive building of red brick with Indiana limestone trim and the "Southern Colonial effect" of its wide porches. It had a 65-bed capacity, with private and semi-private rooms, a few wards and a children's department and nursery.

The first annual report makes interesting reading. During that year, the hospital admitted 1,318 patients—300 from Cornwall, 378 from Newburgh, two from Cuba! There were 732 operations performed, 157 births, 118 ambulance calls. The rates ranged from $4.50 to $10 a day; maternity cases (staying for ten days) were charged $55; the first visit to the clinics—dental and pediatric—cost fifty cents, thereafter a quarter. The patients were cared for by a staff of dedicated doctors and nurses.

The list of donations amply confirms the community's pride in its new hospital. The monetary contributions seem modest by today's standards, but the outpouring of other gifts took up several pages of the report. There were flowers and food, books and magazines, a fish tank for the children's ward, surgical dressings, place cards and Christmas decorations, sandwiches for the medical meetings, even three deer! All of these donations were made in acknowledgement of a generous deed.

On the right hand side of the hospital lobby, in the wooden paneling above the display case, the following words are inscribed:

"In Memory of Ethel Louise Benedict."

Have you ever noticed this inscription and are you aware of the story behind it? How many of the hundreds of people who trooped through the hospital on the opening weekend realized that Ethel Louise Benedict was the little girl to whom Dr. Stillman referred in his speech? She was the daughter of Ray Benedict, an employee of the Stillman Stillwood Farm, who lived with his family in a cottage on the place. Ethel, age six, died in 1919 and was buried on May 16th in Willow Dell Cemetery. The next time you enter the Cornwall Hospital by the front door, stop and read the inscription. Think of the tragedy of Ethel Benedict's death; and remember, too, the man whose compassion inspired a deed which has benefited countless numbers of people.

April 10, 1991
November 1, 1995

45

Captain Thomas Taft
*Slide collection of the
Cornwall Public Library*

Leo A. Fanning
Slide collection of the Cornwall Public Library

Tom Taft
*Slide collection of the
Cornwall Public Library*

Photographs of Cornwall

Dr. Ralph Waldo Thompson   Brig. Gen. Milton F. Davis   Dr. Ernest G. Stillman
Slide collection of the Cornwall Public Library

Memorial Day, 1920, occasion of the World War I cannon presentation.
Cornwall Town Archives

World War I Parade in Newburgh, N.Y.
July 4, 1918
Cornwall Town Archives

Firth Carpet Company around 1900.
Cornwall Town Archives

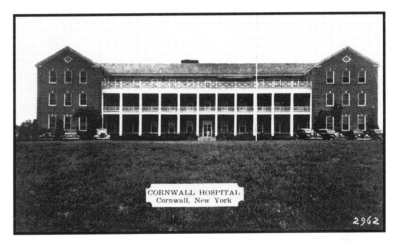

Cornwall Hospital
Cornwall Town Archives

Regional Rural Association Headquarters, Mountainville, N.Y.
Slide collection of the Cornwall Public Library

Store of C.E. Cocks and Sons
Slide collection of the Cornwall Public Library

The Brick Chapel, home of several
Cornwall congregations.
Cornwall Town Archives

The Old Homestead (Sands-Ring House)
Cornwall Town Archives

A Memorial Day Parade.
Slide collection of the Cornwall Public Library

Looking down Dock Hill.
Cornwall Town Archives

Cornwall Landing
Cornwall Town Archives

Mead and Taft Plant after the fire of 1911.
Cornwall Town Archives

CHANGES

In this section one can follow the transformation of Cornwall from a century ago to around 1930— thirty-five years of rapid change. Some of the modern conveniences we take for granted were nonexistent at the turn of the century, and each succeeding decade brought new technological advances to revolutionize America's—and Cornwall's— style of living. The appearance of the town changed, too, as housing developments carved up the large estates and the streets were widened and paved to accommodate the ever-increasing volume of automobile traffic. Cornwall also felt the impact of the social movements then sweeping the country, such as woman suffrage and prohibition. New types of recreation replace the croquet, the euchre parties and the "smokers" enjoyed by a previous generation. Life in the 1930s was a very different experience from living in the Gay Nineties.

Cornwall in 1896

What was Cornwall like a century ago? This survey of the town is based on the town directory of 1896 and issues of *The Cornwall Local*. A comparison with the present is left to the reader.

In those days communities were more self-contained than today; as shown by the directory listings, most of the townspeople's needs could be supplied at home. Dressmakers and tailors made clothes and altered them to fit changes in figure or fashion. Shoe stores sold boots and shoes; three shoemakers were kept busy repairing them. A Chinese laundry cleaned and starched the detachable collars and cuffs then in style for men's shirts. Ready-made clothes could be purchased at Cornwall's four drygoods stores.

With supermarkets far in the future, a number of specialty stores sold meat, fish, baked goods and general groceries—eighteen food stores are listed in the directory! Many households supplemented their food supply by a vegetable garden, a few chickens and a cow. Healthy plants were supplied by two nurseries and several stores sold feed for livestock.

Cornwall had four stage lines to transport passengers between Cornwall and Newburgh, then a thriving metropolis. An important part of their business was carrying the mail from the train depots to the six local post offices. Horses could be boarded or hired at several town livery stables. The liverymen also met the trains and were available to take passengers around town. Bicycles were also very popular, both for transportation and recreation.

A walk along Cornwall's principal streets —Hudson and Main—would make apparent the many business places listed in the directory: drug stores, barber shops (six), jewelers and watch makers, confectionery stores which also sold tobacco products and newspapers; there were also real estate offices, tinsmiths, blacksmiths and harness makers. Cornwall had two lawyers and six doctors, whose offices were located on the main streets, as were many of the hotels and year-round hostelries. The largest industries are listed: Firth Carpet Company, Mead and Taft, the Hedges Brick Yard and the Coal Docks, the last three at Cornwall Landing.

With the new century only four years away, Cornwall was beginning to enjoy the effects of modern technology. The directory lists the Cornwall Electric Lighting and Power Company, which lighted the streets at night and promoted the installation of electricity in homes and business places. The Cornwall Telephone Company was providing service to the community although a home phone was still considered a luxury. The new water supply system supplied running water; to have your house "plumbed"—equipped with indoor bathroom and running water in the kitchen—was becoming more frequent; another convenience was a coal-burning furnace to heat the entire house.

The town newspaper, then as now, was *The Cornwall Local*, selling for one dollar a year. Here is a sample of news taken at random from 1896. Charles Ketcham of Mountainville was then supervisor of the town and Henry D. Lewis the town clerk. That March, Captain Henry Reveley was elected the village president (mayor). Ice skating was good that winter: "There are two rings already cleared on the river for skating." The town's many organizations began the year by installing new officers. Among the church news were items that the Baptists were considering electrifying their place of worship and the Methodist Church had closed for renovations; the Mountainville ladies were holding a jubilee party, perhaps to show off the new pew cushions in their church.

Two school districts decided to consolidate—No. 5 in Canterbury annexing No. 1, a one-room school at the south end of Mill Street. Henceforth, the Firthcliffe children of primary grade age would go to the Mill Street school while their older brothers and sisters had to trudge the length of Willow Avenue to the school on Clinton Street. A January article stressed the importance of joining the Horse Thief Detecting Society to take advantage of the group's assistance in the recovery of stolen horses and detection of the culprits.

February brought a flurry of social events: a brilliant reception at N.Y.M.A. attended by one hundred and fifty guests; a children's operetta at the Baptist Church, a minstrel show for the benefit of the Cornwall Cornet Band, which needed new uniforms, and a concert on the new organ of the Cornwall Presbyterian Church. The newly-formed Cornwall Landing Hose Company, No. 1 now had eighteen members; a delegation journeyed to New York City to purchase hose and other firemanic equipment.

In March a fund was started to provide a drinking fountain for the Village Square in Cornwall-on-Hudson. Canterbury followed suit and, to the chagrin of the lower village, soon had a watering trough and drinking fountain in place at the corner of Willow Avenue and Main Street while the originators of the plan were still soliciting funds. The chief events of the spring were a young people's dance in the Smith House parlors and a concert by the Cornwall Philharmonic Society. The paper praised those merchants who were placing stone pavements in front of their stores. In an era when everyone walked, it is strange that sidewalks were not a public responsibility. Instead of automobile accidents, the milkman's team ran away, strewing the road with milk cans and a quantity of milk.

Arbor Day was observed in May at the "Opera House Rink" on Duncan Avenue; *The Local* commented on the need for another public hall Red Men's Hall was then being erected in Canterbury. Four new ice cream parlors opened on Main Street —a sure sign of approaching summer. A play and concert were part of the commencement festivities at N.Y.M.A., and the 5th Annual Wild Flower Show took place at the Storm King Club[1] on Deer Hill Road. "Have you had the mumps?"asked *The Local* of May 28th. "If not, come to West Cornwall [Firthcliffe] and get them."

Another sign of warm weather: "Mr. Josiah Clark is out again as usual with his

---

1   This organization of a clubhouse and substantial "cottages" was developed by a group of summer residents and operated for a brief period.

wagon full of ice which looks particularly refreshing on these warm days, as it lies piled up, block on block, helter skelter, in cool beautiful profusion."

Highlights of June 1896 were two concerts: the first by the Cornwall Cornet Band, resplendent in their new uniforms; the second, the ambitious presentation of an oratorio "The Holy City" by the Cornwall Philharmonic Society.

There was no Independence Day Celebration that year, but one can be sure that sporadic explosions of firecrackers erupted all over town and the evening sky was illuminated with fireworks displays put on by some of the townspeople. July *Locals* mention the large quantities of raspberries and currants being shipped to city markets— this area was well-suited to the growing of small fruits. Then there was a bicycle trip by three local wheelmen, who traveled to Newburgh one Sunday, crossed the river by ferry, went north to Poughkeepsie and on to Millbrook, where they had dinner, then home by train and ferry.

Now that school was out, the Baptist Boys Brigade Camp opened for the summer at Orrs Mills; the hotels and boarding houses were filled—new arrivals listed each week in *The Local*. School news was prominent. The Alumni Association of District No. 4 (Cornwall-on-Hudson) had a meeting for which Miss Eliza McClean, a retired teacher, composed a poem. The school, located in the rear wing of the present building on Idlewild Avenue, was so overcrowded that immediate action had to be taken. The outcome of the annual meeting was reported in *The Newburgh Telegram*: "Last Thursday night's school meeting was a typical one in Cornwall, one or two bulldozed the meeting and the majority refused to vote." Of the forty-three votes cast, twenty-nine favored an eight thousand dollar appropriation for a new addition to the school. The Board of Education lost no time in publishing the specifications and awarding the contract to Harvey R. Taylor, whose mill bordered Canterbury Creek at Willow Avenue. By the end of July work had begun on a three-story building to adjoin the existing school on the Idlewild Avenue side. While the new school was under construction, the No. 5 school on Clinton Street was also

being enlarged, but not as extensively.

In those days, fairs were a chief summer diversion and a popular form of fund raising. The most unusual fair of 1896 was a Gypsy Camp, arranged by the Cornwall Presbyterian Church and held at Palmer Square, a vacant lot behind the present library. The attendants were dressed as gypsies; there were fortune tellers, exotic foods, and entertainment of gypsy melodies and dances. The motif seems somewhat at odds with the staid sponsoring organization, but it was sure to attract attention and bring out a throng of curious people. Among the more traditional summer amusements were picnics, a play, performances by a touring theatrical company, and a Hudson River Moonlight Excursion. More people were traveling now, especially by railroad. Cornwall's well-known shoemaker, Nicholas Chatfield, Jr. made news by taking off for Cape Cod to visit his brother, Thomas. On the somber side, numerous cases of dog poisoning occurred that summer, and several little children died of "cholera infantum," a vague term used for intestinal complaints.

Labor Day brought an evacuation of the boarding houses as the summer guests returned to their city homes. The schools opened; G.H. Baskerville, the principal of No. 4, had to cope for the first month with an unfinished building. Politics dominated the fall scene. The Republicans organized a McKinley-Hobart Club and hung a large banner across the main street. They held a rally, also a parade— "Our town put on holiday attire last Tuesday evening, when the big Republican parade occurred." Forming at Cornwall Landing, where they were joined by groups coming from Newburgh by boat, the marchers proceeded through the village to Canterbury and West Cornwall. Such spectacles tended to overshadow the efforts of the Democrats, the minority party in town.

Summer amusements were now replaced by other activities: a ball sponsored by the Red Men, another by the Foresters,and a third by the Cornwall Landing Hose Company. No wonder a dancing class opened, with instruction for adults as well as children. The Horse Thief Detecting Society held its annual dinner, the Baptists raised $23.33 at a donation party for their pastor, and Rev. George D.

Egbert of the Canterbury Presbyterian Church started a series of illustrated travelogues. Early in November dedicatory exercises took place to mark the completion of the construction at both schools. The programs were sensibly scheduled on the same day for the convenience of the Albany official who was the speaker. With better facilities and a growing enrollment, each school would soon be eligible to offer high school courses—a big step forward.

Although the Firth Carpet Company occasionally closed briefly when work was slack, there seems to have been plenty of jobs in other fields: Mead and Taft Company was building a mansion for Mrs. Gazzam at the top of Duncan Avenue; W.H. Garrison, another builder, had the contract for five houses in Matthiessen Park. Henry Hunter's livery business took up so much of his time that he had to resign from his mail job, which entailed five round trips each day from the railroad station carrying sixty pouches of mail. From the December issues, it is apparent that Christmas was for the children. Each Sunday School had an entertainment in which the children participated, after which they received from Santa an orange, a book and a box of candy. Their parents celebrated the joyous occasion at music-filled services.

The December 17th issue of *The Local* carried a festively designed page entitled "St. Nick's Advice" sponsored by a dozen Cornwall merchants. Here are some of the products advertised for Christmas:

H.L. Barton - souvenirs made of wood from Storm King Mountain.

Orr and Heman's Poultry Yards - thorougbred poultry.

The Local - a subscription for half price - 50¢ a year.

R.S. Talbot's & Sons - Imperial mincemeat for 8 cents a package.

W.H. & G.B. Mailler's Market - turkeys.

C.E. Cocks & Sons - "the Downtown Grocers" - dealers in Reliable Brands.

Wm. Orr & Sons - "Save Money for Your Christmas Presents - By buying our Coal. The pure stuff, without clinkers. It will Roast the Turkey to a Turn."

J.J. Hall Sons - "Holiday Goods are here." Oranges, Lemons, Grapes, Bananas, Figs, Dates, Raisins, Cocoanuts, Mixed Table Nuts, Plum Pudding, Mince Meat and a variety of Cakes."

January 10, 1996
January 24, 1996

Associations

Suppose you were living in the days before radio and television, and at a time when there were only a few cars—no sports programs to watch, no soap operas, talk shows or Sesame Street; what was there to do? At the turn of the century you would have depended, for recreation and entertainment, on the fraternal lodges, athletic clubs, music and dramatic groups, and on the civic clubs, which worked for community betterment. Cornwall supported an incredible number of such groups — this article will mention a few.

Each of the several churches had its institutions: Sunday School and youth clubs for the young people; Ladies' Aid and Men's Clubs—under various names—for their parents. A high point of the summer for children was the Sunday School picnic. At first an informal affair, it later became an ecumenical function held at the new Bear Mountain Park. The adult organizations existed to aid the church; their fund-raisers in the form of cake and apron sales, suppers and ice cream festivals, fairs, lectures and stereopticon shows, provided a ready source of entertainment.

The schools, too, had their clubs: literary and debating societies, athletic clubs to raise funds for their teams. The Camp Fire Girls dates from the early 1900s; *The Local* reported on their hikes and campouts as well as meetings and projects. Rev. Hugh K. Fulton of the Canterbury Presbyterian Church led a Boy Scout Troop and Cornwall had a branch of the Y.M.C.A. The most outstanding youth organization was the Garden Athletic Club, which grew from a band of boys who raised vegetables to sell for athletic projects, to the construction of a gym. Although a girls' basketball team was no longer a novelty, most of the sports organizations were for men. The Firthcliffe Club was a community center for that part of town. The Firth basketball team was followed in the spring by a baseball team, both of which maintained a busy schedule of games. Bowlers could use the club alleys; sometimes they challenged bowlers from the lower village, who met at Thompson's alleys on Hudson Street. This facility was also the winter quarters of the Cornwall Rifle Club when the members could not practice on an outdoor shooting range. The Cornwall-on-Hudson baseball teams played on the field behind the modern elementary school.

Agricultural societies flourished. The Mountainville Grange was the largest. In its own building (still standing on Route 32), the members met for weekly meetings, seasonal entertainments and a Labor Day clambake. Some years the Grange sponsored lectures by experts from the Cornell Agricultural School. The Cornwall Poultry Association was another active society; to encourage the raising of unusual breeds, it held an annual poultry show with prizes awarded in various categories. Several young men organized a Homing Pigeon Society, which trained the birds and challenged other pigeon fanciers to races.

The fraternal lodges were among the most popular of the Cornwall associations. Jerusalem Temple Lodge of Masons was the oldest. Formed early in the 19th century, it died out, then was reorganized in the 1870s. The Knights of Pythias and the Odd Fellows each had its adherents and a women's auxiliary. The Clan MacLeod and the Gleniffer Lodge,

Daughters of Scotia, were composed of those with Scottish roots. The Waoroneck Tribe, Improved Order of Red Men, was one of the largest of the lodges. Its lasting contribution was the erection of a building, Red Men's Hall, which served for many years as a community center.

The first civic organizations were the fire companies: Highland Engine, formed in the 1830s, and Storm King Engine, a few decades later. Each group built an engine house with quarters for fire apparatus and clubrooms. Each group held an annual fair, which drew a large crowd. The Cornwall Civic Organization sponsored lectures and served as a forum for important local issues. An annual banquet, held at N.Y.M.A., was a prestigious event. The Emslie Post, G.A.R., a forerunner of the American Legion, was a society of Civil War veterans. On Memorial Day the men decorated the graves of their fallen comrades and took part in the parade and other patriotic observances.

Musical societies were another source of recreation. The two village bands were performing summer concerts as early as the 1880s. Later, the Firthcliffe Band superseded the Cornwall group, playing one night in the Cornwall Bandstand, another night in Firthcliffe. Court Storm King of the American Foresters had a fife and drum corps, which often accompanied local marching units. There were also choral societies and orchestras, short-lived ventures which met for a season or two then disbanded.

Among the women's organizations was the Ingleside, a literary society whose members prepared papers on selected topics, and the Village Improvement Society of Cornwall-on-Hudson followed by its counterpart in Canterbury. The two joined forces to preserve the decaying old building, known today as the Sands-Ring House. Later came the Cornwall Suffrage Club, led by a number of intrepid women who campaigned for the women's vote. Instead of wondering what to do, Cornwallites of an earlier generation had the problem of choosing among a variety of activities, and all without leaving town.

February 5, 1992

57

The Movies

"Something Entirely New!" exclaimed a headline. "Moving pictures and reproductions from life will be exhibited at an entertainment in the Library Hall on Thursday evening, December 30th by the Hatch Electro-Photo Co. of New York City.... Among other things, a wonderful exhibition is given of the 'Black Diamond' Express moving at a rate of 60 miles an hour... no one should miss it who can possibly attend." Thirty-five different scenes would be shown by means of a Projectoscope. Could that audience of 1897 have envisioned the expansion of the motion picture industry into America's foremost entertainment?

Such shows must have been rare in Cornwall, for the next reported performance was in 1900—a moving picture "exhibition" for the high school benefit fund. It was not until 1908 that shows were appearing on a regular basis: "Matthiessen Hall has been rented for moving pictures and illustrated songs Monday evenings" —admission ten and fifteen cents; the dramatization of a story would come later. Occasional ads in *The Cornwall Local* mention special shows for the holidays, such as the American Kinetoscope Company's presentation of illustrated songs on Thanksgiving Day and "High Class Moving Pictures at Matthiessen Hall in December," where one could "Hear the World's Greatest Baritone Singer Mr. Harry Henry of New York City. All New Songs. All New Pictures." These forerunners of the true "talkies" must have synchronized the music with the film.

In 1909 the Knights of Pythias sponsored "The Passion Play" by Powers Motion Pictures, and the following year Matthiessen Hall was filled to the doors for another production by the same company. "The show was a great success, consisting of comedy, light opera, etc.... A new set of Talking Pictures may come again next week." In 1913 the E. & C. Photo Company showed motion pictures in a tent called the Airdome, erected on the present Town Hall grounds; it opened again the next spring on Memorial Day for the showing three nights a week of "high class film productions."

The popularity of motion pictures gave rise to the "nickelodeon," a long, narrow room containing a stage at one end with a white curtain and a piano. The rest of the room was filled with seats for spectators, leaving only enough space at the rear for a projector. Cornwall was fortunate in having several halls suitable for the showing of motion pictures and so escaped the nickelodeons, which were often condemned as fire traps. The Cornwall-on-Hudson High School, which opened in 1924, had an auditorium equipped with a projection booth.

Not only did Cornwall possess halls to serve as movie theaters; it had its own impressario in the person of Edwin Knapp, who handled the booking of motion pictures in addition to his regular job as owner of a feed store. He rented the halls, secured the films, hired a man to run the projector and a pianist, for music was a necessary accompaniment to silent films. Whatever mood was required to highlight a scene—romantic, sinister, tragic, patriotic, martial, humorous, etc.—all could be enhanced by musical selections played by the versatile pianist. *The Local* mentions several pianists: Edna Taylor, who resigned in 1914 at the time of her marriage; Lillian Eckert, and Mrs. Benson Halstead, whose "music for the movies has a variety of catchy new pieces and ... [whose] touch is quickly distinguished." She was obviously a favorite.

By 1914 movie dramas were being shown: a western, "Ashes of Three" and "Shenandoah," a Civil War story; also "The Ruins of Pompeii." In 1916 there was "The Juggernaut," the first Blue Ribbon Vitagraph film to be shown in Cornwall. Although Manager Knapp seems to have made an effort to obtain the best movies, and was generous in donating some of the proceeds to worthy causes, a letter in *The Local* accused him of corrupting the youth of the town. "What good are the public school and the church and all of the restraining and enobling influences of a community life when the moving pictures of murder, brutality, and seduction are spread before their astonished eyes?" Knapp retorted that his one great desire was to secure bigger, better and cleaner pictures, and he contended that 95% of his films were "good, clean stories." When he discovered the critic was a member of the town clergy, Knapp sent him a free pass to the movies.

As the movie industry burgeoned, many refinements were introduced. The dramatization of stories called for able actors, movie stars whose glamorous lives made good publicity and increased the box office receipts. The public interest in current events led to the showing of news films. In 1911 scenes of the Italo-Turkish War could be viewed as well as such local events as the Volunteer Firemen's parade. On the occasion of the presentation to Cornwall of the captured World War I cannon, Dr. Ernest G. Stillman was on hand to film the event. Some years later, a Cornwall movie was produced for the benefit of the American Legion.

The Local's Coming Events column now listed the current movies and Manager Knapp ran ads for special shows. When the program became longer, with a news reel and a short comedy or other feature in addition to the main film, the prices escalated to thirty cents for adults and twenty cents for children.

In the early years of film production, before Hollywood became the center of the industry, many movies were made on the east coast. A scene for one was filmed in Cornwall, the details of which were reported by *The Local* of March 17, 1921.

"The Fox Film Company of New York made three attempts to stage a dynamite destruction of a bridge... in Mountainville. Monday afternoon one hundred automobiles and one thousand people waited for a long time while the crew of the Fox Company prepared for the destruction of a bridge which their engineers had erected. Finally everything was ready and the signal given to blow the bridge to atoms. People were warned to stand back. Everybody held their breath. The automobile moved across the bridge and there was a crash but no explosion. It was intended that the dynamite would explode and the bridge break down exactly at the same second, but it didn't, so they built the bridge again Tuesday and exploded it Wednesday afternoon and the picture was complete. They took many scenes from about that section of town and are expected here again during the summer.... The title of the movie was "The Thunder."

"The Lion and the Mouse," a talkie starring Lionel Barrymore, appeared at the Broadway Theater in Newburgh, July, 1928, spelling an end to the showing of silent films.

The demolition of Matthiessen Hall in 1934 paved the way for the town's first real movie house, the Storm King Theatre, which was built on the site. Here a past generation of Cornwallites attended the movies, and their offspring, replete with popcorn, enjoyed the Saturday matinees.

May 3, 1995

The Automobile

The impact of the automobile on Cornwall during the first quarter of the present century was a process that was being duplicated all across the country. The first appearance of an auto, as reported by *The Cornwall Local,* was in the spring of 1900 when Dr. Horace Reynolds, a Tarrytown dentist, drove to Cornwall to visit relatives. Two years later, a couple vacationing at the Grand View House brought along their "fine large auto." The following summer, "a large and formidable auto" was spotted in Mountainville, which aroused a curiosity similar to sighting a rare bird. The word "car" had not yet entered the vocabulary; the vehicle was referred to as an automobile or auto. When an endurance test of autos was expected to pass through Cornwall, enroute from New York to Pittsburgh by way of Buffalo, the owners of spirited horses were warned to keep them off the highway. A subsequent newspaper item revealed that twenty-five out of thirty-four autos had completed the trip, and added that the experience had been an endurance test for the drivers as well.

Forty-four cars were counted passing through Mountainville on Memorial Day,

1905. About this time, an intrepid motorist drove over the mountain to West Point; whether the auto remained unscathed after the trip on this notoriously rugged, winding road is not of record. By 1910 a few local people had invested in an auto, the purchase duly noted in *The Local*. On the streets of Cornwall could be seen a Stevens-Duryea, a Reo Roadster, a 30 H.P. Abbott-Detroit, a Buick, Michigan Roadster, Studebaker and several Fords. The summer residents started to bring automobiles to Cornwall for the season, hiring a young local fellow as chauffeur and mechanic—the early cars were subject to frequent breakdowns. Albert R. Ledoux of Deer Hill Road was having his coachman take "chauffeur instructions." His neighbor, Mr. Pagenstecher, invested in a Belgian car of solid mahogany costing $7,500, but when he found it unable to make the hills, he exchanged it for a Mercedes. One of the first two-car families owned an Overland "runabout" for delivery purposes and a 5-passenger touring car for pleasure. The summer of 1915 a law went into effect in New York State regulating motor vehicle registration, brakes, lights, signals, etc. The speed limit for towns was set at 15 m.p.h.—before then it had been 8 m.p.h. in Cornwall!

The urge to own an automobile resulted in new types of business: auto agencies to sell cars and garages to service them—often run by the same individual and frequently located in a former livery stable. Harry Hancon opened the Cornwall Garage on Main Street in 1911, selling it a few years later to Harry E. Keevill, one of his employees. The business prospered; there was an increasing number of cars to repair and the sale of Chevrolets and Willys-Knights was brisk. After the war Keevill opened an annex in the lower village. Another garage was located on the site of the present B.C. and M. Garage; Samuel Van Tassell had one in Cornwall-on-Hudson near the Square, also James Lewis who had the Ford agency. One could tank up at these garages or at gas pumps installed in front of grocery stores. In 1912 a motorist made a round trip to New York City in one day—his mileage of nineteen miles to the gallon was considered very good. That year Charles C. Cocks of the firm of C.E. Cocks' Sons bought

his first car, a Ford; soon the store was converting from horse-drawn delivery wagons to trucks.

Despite the actions of the state legislature to enact uniform motor vehicle laws and the efforts of Constable George Toombs and his successor, Leo Fanning, to enforce them, automobile accidents were commonplace. The chief causes seem to have been auto breakdowns, skittish horses, and unskilled drivers. When overtaken by a speeding noisy auto, horses would become frightened and bolt, sometimes overturning the vehicle they were pulling and injuring the occupants. Unwary bicyclists and pedestrians would sometimes be struck down by speeding autos. Thomas W. Weeks of Duncan Avenue was understandably irate when a speeder ran over his pet collie. Many accidents were caused by mechanical problems—brakes failing, blow outs—and by poor drivers whose speeding cars overturned on dangerous curves or collided with other vehicles. The roads had not been built for modern transportation; in snowy weather, motorists had to resort to horse and sleigh.

In 1915 Officer Toombs arrested a "speed maniac" who tore down Hudson Street at 70 m.p.h., swung into Cliffside Park and careened over the bank. The car was wrecked, but the driver was unhurt! Young men took naturally to cars; their over-confidence, however, caused many of the speeding accidents. There was no such thing as driver instruction, but by 1922, *The Local* ran a series of articles on the upkeep of autos.

The automobile continued to create new jobs. Michael Gogarty, a former blacksmith, started a taxi business, one of several in town. These first taxis were open cars to which rubberized side curtains could be fastened in bad weather. In 1915 Gilbert MacMorran bought a Ford; with this car and a 7-passenger Studebaker he could "offer Firthcliffe residents comfortable traveling facilities." His neighbors preferred this method of travel between Cornwall and Newburgh to buses. The only trouble was that MacMorran's franchise was for a bus, a fact which caused friction between him and the Newburgh City Council. According to *The Local*, his license was constantly being revoked, but somehow the Firthcliffers continued to ride in his cars.

For years, George E. Davis and Sons had run horse-drawn stages to Newburgh; now they refitted the stage onto an auto body, and by 1916, they were operating three "auto stages," one of which was equipped with electric push buttons, heat, and a side entrance. Other early buses were run by Speder, Schwab and Brunton. A man named Huggins had an early morning bus for students attending school in Newburgh; another took workers to and from the Newburgh Shipyards, where a large number of Cornwall men were employed.

By the 1920s, *The Cornwall Local* contained many ads for used cars: Cornwall families were turning in their first cars for a new one. The automobile was here to stay.

July 20, 1994

Housing Developments

Housing projects, a familiar phenomenon of recent times, date from the 1890s. Matthiessen Park might be considered Cornwall's first housing development. The name came from an early owner, Erard A. Matthiessen, whose deed of 1863 for sixteen acres included a large house on a bluff overlooking the river. Entering from Idlewild Avenue, the approach to the mansion was along a winding driveway; other drives led to the barns, stable, carriage house, wagon shed, ice house, etc. There were plantings of ornamental trees and shrubs, orchards, and greenhouses filled with exotic plants. When Mr. Matthiessen moved to a house he had built off Deer Hill Road on the mountain, he adapted his estate in the village for the betterment of the community. To his former home came children from the nearby public school—the boys for classes in mechanical arts, the girls for sewing and cooking. Next he turned to the construction of houses which would be rented at a reasonable price. The first five of these "cottages" were situated along one edge of the property—on Pine Street. The venture proved so popular that he built ten larger houses, five on Pine Street with lots adjoining another five on Spruce Street.

The houses were well-designed and well-built. The architect was Adam Jaeger, son of Paul Jaeger, a long-time manager of the Matthiessen property. The firm of Mead and Taft built some of the houses; the other contractor was William H. Garrison. The cottages had wide piazzas with a balcony above, hardwood floors, fireplaces, modern plumbing and heating. The lots were 90 x 100 feet, "affording plenty of room for croquet, tennis and other out-of-doors games." An elaborate sewer system took care of the entire estate. Matthiessen Park, as it was now called, was a most desirable place to live; among the tenants were a hotel manager, physician, lawyer, school principal and other substantial citizens.

In October 1913, eight years after Mr. Matthiessen's death, all fifteen houses were sold at auction. A full-page ad in *The Cornwall Local* heralded the three-day event, exhorting home-seekers: "Here is your chance to own your own home in one of the most delightful spots on the Hudson River." "All Houses Sold," reported a headline of the following week. The article went on to list the purchaser for each property and the price, which varied from $1,600 to $2,600. The Matthiessen cottages have undergone changes, both inside and out, over the years, but all are standing. The mansion was less fortunate: a boarding house, then Braden's Preparatory School for West Point and Annapolis, it stood vacant for a time before being demolished in 1974.

Cliffside Park, an estate at the other end of the village, was a larger development. An early owner was David Carson, whose Italianate-style mansion dates from about 1850. Ten years later he sold the property to Albert Palmer, a New Jersey businessman; and for almost fifty years, the Palmer family made Cliffside their summer home. Old maps show the house in the center of the estate, reached from Hudson Street by circuitous drives, one of which led to outbuildings near Dock Hill. Since the family was in residence for less than half the year, townspeople regarded Cliffside as a public park —"an inviting spot for lovers' rambles" and for "unexcelled river and Highland views." In 1887, veterans of the Civil War's Orange Blossoms Regiment held an encampment there; and in 1909 Cornwallites lined the bluff to witness the festivities of the Hudson-Fulton Celebration.

Albert Palmer died in 1893, his wife Cornelia in 1904, after which the property was sold. In 1910 it changed hands again, bought by Dayton Hedges of Long Island. In September of that year, Hedges placed a large ad in the Cornwall newspaper, advertising "a golden opportunity"—a public auction of lots at Cliffside Park. Two weeks later the paper listed the first purchasers, some of whom bought several lots. The following week: "James G. Dwyer has purchased several building lots ... and will erect a number of $3,000 houses ..."

Building started at once. By November "Miss Jennie Jackson's new house is nearly completed. It is not far from the entrance...and is quite a cozy looking little 'nest'." The paper of November 24th carried an announcement of the formation of a Cliffside Park Association, and an article entitled "What Cornwall Has To Be Thankful For" by James G. Dwyer, who combined the compatible occupations of builder and developer. He cited employment opportunities, good roads and local government, but obviously the most important item to his way of thinking was the new development: he predicted that $100,000 would be spent on housing within the coming year.

"An atmosphere teeming with activity is noticeable at Cliffside Park these days, where preparations for new buildings and various other improvements are seen on every side." Adam B. Jaeger was erecting a colonnaded pavilion at the end of the cliff; the surroundings, "tastefully laid out" and lit by electricity, would make it "a veritable beauty spot." Roads were being graded by "the bustling young contractor," Thomas O'Neill, and spread with ten carloads of crushed stone. Large rustic piers were placed at the park

entrance, adorned by electric lamps and the name of the development. Along Grand View Avenue were the homes of William H. and George D. Mailler, Frank E. Vickere and William Briggs. Mrs. Young's house stood at the entrance, reached by a flight of concrete steps; Dwyer's bungalows were probably those on the east side of Hedges Avenue. The residence of G. E. DeGroat was near the pavilion and the Palmer mansion was being renovated by Major Chancellor B. Martin.

A walk through Cliffside Park is a good way to observe how the estate developed. The once parklike appearance has been lost in a welter of dense housing. Interspersed among the original homes are those of a later architectural style, crowded onto properties which once contained several lots. Some of the earlier houses have been modernized; Grand View Avenue has been extended to meet Wilson Road. All that remains of the original Cliffside Park are the mansion, now an apartment house, and the unsurpassed views.

The next development, advertised as Cornwall Gardens, dates from the 1930s; everyone called it the Weeks Estate, and so it is known today. The first mention in the press was on August 8, 1929: an announcement that the 50-acre estate of the late T.W. Weeks was to be developed into "a very desirable restricted residential park ... one of the most beautiful and picturesque sites in the Hudson Valley." The next item stated that title had passed to the Cornwall Realty Development Company and that Harry A. Wilson was the agent.

The Weeks Estate comprised several parcels. The original purchase on Duncan Avenue had been made in 1869, when James W. Smith acquired 7.5 acres from Julia W.H. George, the price of $12,000 indicating a house on the site. Smith, president of the Consolidated Gas Company of New York, made Cornwall his summer home for the next twenty-five years, and during this period increased his holdings to include much of the old Duncan farm as well as acreage from adjoining land owners. After his death in 1894, the property came into the possession of a relative, Thomas W. Weeks. Weeks, also a summer resident, is remembered for his philanthropy, especially to the Blind Home.

When he died in the spring of 1929, his executors sold the Cornwall property and within a year the development was underway.

Edward B. Stoddard installed the water mains—his family would later come to live there—then came roads and electricity. There were to be two sections: five 1½-acre lots in front of the Weeks mansion, the rest to be divided into lots of 20 x 100 feet—each building site to consist of three lots with a frontage of sixty feet. The streets were named for Cornwall celebrities: Willis for Nathaniel P. Willis of Idlewild, Barr for Amelia E. Barr, Roe for Edward P. Roe—all writers; Stillman for the prominent family, two of whose homes were nearby, and Weeks for the former owner.

Construction soon began. The houses built during the next decade reflect the architectural styles then popular—Tudor, colonial, ranch, Cape Cod. Profiting possibly from Cliffside Park whose lots were very small, the developers sited each house on a generous plot. Ten acres went to the Blind Home and ten more, (including the mansion) to Harvey V. Duell, which cancelled the plans to subdivide near the house. It is interesting to note that each of these first developments preserved the original house on the property.

April 17, 1991
March 4, 11, 1992

Woman Suffrage

The ratification of the 19th amendment to the Constitution occurred seventy-five years ago—on August 18, 1920. This action, the culmination of a movement which had been gathering stength over the years, gave American women the right to vote. Here is an account of how a handful of Cornwall women played a small part in achieving this far-reaching legislation.

In the spring of 1912, fifteen thousand women had marched in a Suffragette Parade which was reported in *The Cornwall Local*: "In a harlequin uniformed parade which unfolded its beribboned length along Fifth Avenue in New York woman suffrage marched in the most significant demonstration ever attempted by it in this country." Despite the "variegated color scheme" of the participants, the order and decorum of their ranks came as a surprise to the tens of thousands massed along the line of march.

The article does not mention whether any Cornwall women marched in this parade, but some were doubtless among the spectators and all were made aware of the eventful occasion by the newspaper reports.

A few days later Cornwall held its own demonstration—an open air suffragette meeting in the Village Square, described in *The Local* as "a brand new sensation." From the bandstand in the center of the Square, Miss Nettie Podell of the New York State Suffrage Association spoke to a crowd of two hundred. Despite her lengthy speech, lasting two hours, "perfect order was maintained," and fifty-three supporters signed up, among them Mrs. Bartley G. Furey, Miss Mary A. Cocks and Mrs. Sidney Sherwood, all of whom pledged to assist in the organization of a local suffrage group. One month later, eleven women met at the Angola Road home of Mrs. Sherwood and the Cornwall Equal Suffrage Club came into being. Thereafter, the group met regularly at the Cornwall Library; a year later the enrollment had doubled. Its activities were reported in the columns of *The Local*: in addition to recruiting new members, the club sent a contribution to the Suffrage Parade in Washington, D.C. and sponsored a meeting at which the president of the State Suffrage Club was the speaker.

In 1914 the president of the local club was Mrs. Henry Lyle Winter, the wife of Dr. Winter, whose sanitarium then occupied the site of the Town Hall parking lot. That year the group had a booth at the Businessmen's Picnic, and in November they sponsored a Grand Suffrage Rally at Red Men's Hall. The speech by Mrs. Vanamee, a well-known suffragist, was followed by remarks from male supporters: Dr.

Winter, Henry W. Chadeayne (an attorney and former town supervisor), and Lawrence F. Abbott. The latter explained that a study of countries where equal suffrage prevailed had converted him to the cause.

In 1915 Red Men's Hall was again the scene of a mass meeting, and that year a delegation from Orange County attended the Suffrage Parade in New York City. This time Cornwall was represented—Mrs. Sherwood's four daughters, Margaret, Helen, Jean and Penelope, were among the marchers. With a suffrage amendment on the state ballot in November, "the Cornwall Equal Suffrage Club appeals to the voters of the Town of Cornwall to give earnest consideration to the Constitutional Amendment granting the franchise to the women of our state." The amendment did not pass although the Cornwall vote favored equal suffrage by 455 to 393.

In 1916 the Cornwall club attended a district meeting of the State Suffrage Party in the Goshen Court House. The attendees were urged to poll the women in their communities to ascertain their sentiments on the suffrage question.

1917 was a "banner" year. The club was probably responsible for the conspicuous banner across Hudson Street which proclaimed: "1,006,503 women in New York State ask you to vote for women suffrage," and for ads in *The Local*, one of which urged: "Men of New York, Cast Your Votes for Women." A later editorial stated that the Equal Suffrage victory in New York State on Election Day, 1917, "marks an epoch in the state's history."

Cornwall women living in the village were able to vote in the election of March, 1918. Commented *The Local*: "The door is thus happily opened for the women of the Village of Cornwall to cast their first votes for the continuance of good government in this municipality." Seventy-three women went to the polls on this occasion, their names preserved for posterity. In order to vote in the national election that fall, women were required to register—two hundred and eighteen complied.

On Friday, June 21, 1918, the Cornwall Equal Suffrage Club, its goal attained, voted to disband and issued the following statement: "Just eight years ago [six, according to the newspaper] eleven women met ... and organized the club. Although the membership never grew to be more than thirty in number, the club has been very much alive and a great deal has been accomplished in the way of public service by its members.

"As a final message to the women of Cornwall, the Club urges each one to face their responsibility and privilege by using the vote wisely; that our men at the front may come home to pure politics and better laws."

September 13, 1995

No-License

Cornwall citizens turn out on Election Day to cast their votes for town and county officials, for state and congressional legislators, and every four years for a president. In the early years of the present century, our grandparents also voted on the temperance issue—whether Cornwall would be a "wet" or "dry" town for the next two years. Here is a brief history of the temperance movement in Cornwall.

Our first regular newspaper was *The Cornwall Times*, published in the 1870s and 1880s by Miss Sarah J.A. Hussey. Believing Temperance to be "the common cause of humanity," she filled the columns of her paper with predictable topics: sermons on the evils of strong drink, the need to replace the saloon with the coffee room, and Sunday School temperance lessons. With the appearance of a rival town paper in the eighties, the temperance agitation continued, chiefly under the auspices of women and the clergy. "A committee of ladies are circulating a petition to have certain saloons in the village of Canterbury closed, in which it is claimed gambling is allowed, and where it is also claimed liquors are habitually sold to minors." "All Ladies, interested in the Temperance reform, are invited to meet in the Cornwall-on-Hudson Presbyterian Church, Wednesday afternoon, November 16, at 3 o'clock. Interesting speakers ... will be present, and measures will be taken for the organization of a W.C.T.U."[2]

According to a state law, towns voted for excise commissioners, who were empowered to grant licenses for the sale of liquor. A letter of 1881 urged the local Law and Order League to be vigilant as it was rumored that the liquor dealers intended selling drink without applying for a license. It is evident that Cornwall was a very wet town. For a male population of less than one thousand, there were twenty-seven saloons within the town limits, considerably more than we have today. Drunkenness was a common sight and weekend brawls taxed the resources of the lone police officer. Probably it was the combined efforts of temperance propaganda in the press, mass meetings presided over by the town clergy and prominent citizens such as Thomas Taft, and organizations such as the Law and Order League and the Order of Good Templars which resulted in the headlines of March 3, 1892: "No Rum! That's the Verdict." Despite the terrible weather— it had snowed and sleeted all day—fifty conveyances were on hand to transport voters to the single polling place on Main Street, probably the Highland Engine Firehouse. Seven hundred and twenty-three men cast their ballots to vote in Harris B. Cox for excise commissioner. The excise board, now in the hands of anti-liquor men, would grant no liquor licenses in Cornwall. On election day, the W.C.T.U. Ladies had opened a coffee room near the polls; what effect did the two hundred lunches they served have on the outcome?

According to *The Cornwall Local*: "The last days of license were very hilarious ones. Rum was ushered out in boozy fashion." One liquor dealer was heard to say: "Let them go dry for a time and they will sicken of the bargain." Some of the saloons ostensibly closed or converted to tobacco, newspaper and confectionery stores. But with little means of enforcement, there was no difficulty in obtaining a drink, especially when the nearby towns of New Windsor and Newburgh were wet.

The local press kept up its barrage against the Demon Rum, printing statements in favor of no-license by such influential citizens as James Stillman, Lyman Abbott, Albert Ledoux. Henry Hunter, a Cornwall liveryman, expressed the opinion of many of his fellow townsmen: "Having tried the no-license system for one year, I am more than satisfied that no-license for the town means more money for all the necessary things that are needed, better health, more happiness in families, more peace and a sure foundation on which the future prosperity of this town and our business depend."

In response to a petition, the issue could be voted on every other year. Prior to the vote, there would be a number of mass meetings and letters pro and con. Said the wets: "... the no-license fanatics since their rise to power caused the deflection of millions of dollars from the town," their prime example being the decline of the summer tourist business, which they blamed on no-license. Not so, countered the drys, the culprit was the railroads, which opened up new vacation spots and took the summer boarders to the Catskills.

In 1897 the system was changed to direct balloting on liquor licensing, and the date moved from March to Election Day in November. In 1914 one hundred and twenty-four Cornwallites petitioned for a vote on the liquor question. The next issue of *The Local* carried two full columns of a "Mother's Appeal" for no-license, listing the names of several hundred Cornwall women. No-license won that year by a majority of 214. Two years later, when the issue came up again, it was feared that the hotels might be licensed. "A Vote for Hotel License is a Vote for Raines Hotels," thundered *The Local*, and everyone knew what that meant. The Raines Law defined a hotel as containing ten bedrooms or more; by building an addition, a former saloon could qualify as a hotel. But no- license won again in Cornwall.

The last petition before National Prohibition never came to a vote. Suspecting irregu-

---

2 Women's Christian Temperance Union.

larities in the petition, the Law and Order League hired a lawyer to investigate. At a hearing attended by the headmasters of N.Y.M.A.and Storm King School, a delegation from the Firth Carpet Company management, Thomas Taft and Charles C. Cocks, the judge granted an injunction barring the vote.

Two years later came National Prohibition, sanctioned by the passage of the 18th ammendment to the U.S. Constitution. World War I had hastened the support of the move-ment; conservation of grain supplies and rolling stock made it a patriotic issue. The 18th amendment was ratified June 29, 1919 and went into effect on January 20, 1920. Thus culminated a movement which had been under agitation for over a century. The tactics of temperance were not so different from some of our current issues, only television makes today's more pervasive. How will the problems of the 1990s be judged a century hence?

October 27, 1993

The Dance Pavilion

An old timer, recalling Cornwall's "Good Old Days," lamented how little took place in the summer now compared to the profusion of fairs, picnics, dances, band concerts and movies of her youth. The modern scene at the Town Hall Park, where children compete with the wildlife as they indulge in an array of summer programs would seem to belie her statement, but these activities are chiefly for young people.

In the early decades of the present century, there was no Town Hall Park. The Old Homestead, on the opposite side of the street, served as a community center, especially in the summer. The decaying old house, rich in history, had been rescued through the joint efforts of the Village Improvement Societies. After a period of renovation, the house opened with formal ceremonies in 1912. The tea room soon became the fashionable place to take friends for lunch or tea; for a time it was managed by the Misses Taylor, descendants of the Ring family. A 50-cent golf lunch on Saturdays and Sunday evening suppers were features of the 1916 season, and the tearoom was patronized by the New York Military Academy for fraternity suppers and other get-togethers and as a place where cadets could entertain their parents.

The first summer fair featured a pageant of historical tableaux—to remind visitors of the Old Homestead's place in history. The fair became an annual event, the post of chairman invariably held by Mrs. Pauline Sands Lee. The proceeds of these ventures went toward reducing the debt assumed in the purchase of the house and its renovation.

In 1914 a dance pavilion had been erected behind the house. Some objection was made that its close proximity to the Quaker homestead was unfitting, but the prospects of additional revenue prevailed. The importance of dancing in those days can hardly be overstated. Back when Cornwall was a summer resort, the hotels vied in staging elaborate hops and cotillions, to which the town belles were invited. Later, dancing classes were all the rage, each ending the season with a reception and dance. By this time there were a number of assembly halls large enough for the holiday balls—at Easter, Thanksgiving, New Years and Washington's Birthday.

And now the pavilion—ideal for warm weather in contrast to the stuffy, poorly-ventilated halls. Organizations began to rent the pavilion for benefit dances; and weekly dances were instituted, sometimes with an orchestra, at other times to the music of a victrola. A weekly dance series, managed by William E. Ward and John E. Fanning, continued for several summers and drew large crowds, at times over one hundred couples, those from Newburgh coming in an "autobus." Charles E. Rupp's three-piece orchestra provided the music; the charge, thirty-five cents.

"Successful Dance at Pavilion" is a headline from the *Cornwall Press* of May 31, 1917. "The first of the series of dances for the summer season under the management of Messrs. Ward and Fanning ... was most successful, both socially and financially, and the young men feel encouraged with the venture. Rupp's orchestra furnished excellent music and the Misses Taylor served delicious grape punch and home-made cake in the Tea Room. The night was given the name of Pink Night ... and the color scheme of decorations and electric lights corresponded." A list of guests followed, and the program for the next dance—all traditional tunes; jazz had not yet reached Cornwall.

Some of the dances had a theme: Equal Suffrage, Chauffeurs' Night, Red Cross, A Shirtwaist Night, a Lucky Number Dance. Was attendance dropping off at the end of August when a cash door prize was offered? From the August 24th paper: "The Pavilion floor was never in better condition for dancing, the decorations are beautiful and the orchestra is always full of pep. There will be plenty of enjoyment for the older folks as well as the young. Dancing in the open air is a very healthful exercise; so be sure and come Friday evening of this week."

In addition to the dance pavilion, a Girl Scout cabin also occupied a portion of the Old Homestead property. A new and enthusiastic group in the 1920s, the scouts were great fund-raisers; from food sales, a play and dances, they raised half of the $1,200 needed to build their cabin in a single year. While the Girl Scouts were busy with their activities, the Boy Scouts, with Leo A. Fanning as leader, were taking strenuous hikes through the mountains.

From a comparison of the summer events of long ago with those of today, we can conclude that the automobile, the television set and jogging shoes have wrought great changes in America's recreational habits.

August 11, 1993

The Winter of 1923

The year of 1923 is of special interest for it was the first winter that the Storm King Highway was in use. After opening in October, the scenic road attracted heavy traffic, especially on weekends; but winter was a different matter. The West Point traffic of modern times had not yet materialized; only the Storm King buses made daily trips over the highway.

The winter of 1923 was a hard one. According to a railroad official, "...more snow fell up-state during the first two weeks of the new year than during any corresponding period since 1874....conditions this winter are unprecedented," he declared. "...To keep traffic moving on anything like normal schedules the New York Central has detailed more than 100 locomotives to snowplow work."

How did the Storm King Highway fare? The newspapers from that winter recount many problems. January 18: "It is reported that large icicles are hanging from the rocks along the Storm King road and are causing the patrolmen, Frank Diller and Leo Fanning, no small amount of worry. The morning thaw and afternoon freeze causes large icicles to form and it has been suggested that they be shot down with rifles as is done many places in the west." There was also another hazard. "Patrolmen along the Storm King road are keeping watch for pieces of rock which become loosened and slide down the mountainside. Recently a large rock weighing several ton, became dislodged and crashed down the mountain, cutting trees and shrubbery in its path, until it finally landed in the highway against the wall. It required several sticks of dynamite to break it up so it could be thrown over the wall."

January 25: "Snowslides on the Storm

King mountain forced the Storm King Stage Corporation to suspend trips Sunday, the slides being occasioned by the rain which set in as an accompaniment to the January thaw. The first of the important slides took place on Saturday evening and the bus line was forced to resort to men with shovels to clear the track for the vehicles. Later in the night there were other and larger slides which brought down such a volume of snow that it was impossible to make trips on Sunday. The buses are now running on regular schedule again."

By February it was becoming increasingly difficult to keep the road open. Harry Hancon, the town commissioner of highways, had a snowplow and a large force of men at work there, while another crew was shoveling at the West Point end. The bus company had trouble finding shovelers after the latest storm although they were offering "big money." Two huge army trucks attempted to get through, but became stalled. "It required the services of a small army of shovelers several hours to release the trucks and get them through .... Officers Diller and Fanning, of the interstate police, report that numerous slides have taken place…bringing down many dead trees and brush, which makes it almost impossible for autos to pass at times."

Another snowslide occurred early in March, completely filling the road for 25-30 feet. A one-way track was with difficulty shoveled through the obstruction. The morning patrol reported no problem, but by afternoon the highway was again blocked. Commented *The Press*: "Both officers agree that had a car been caught at this point serious damage might have resulted." None of the euphoric predictions of the benefits Cornwall would reap from the Storm King Highway took into account the dangers of winter travel along the mountainside.

Now that travel by automobile was commonplace, town streets also had to be kept open. *The Cornwall Press* praised the town and village road superintendents "for the excellent care they have given our roads this winter." The village trustees had a 2½-ton truck with plow attachment demonstrated on Mountain Road and were so impressed with the results that they decided to purchase it. But when the proposition was presented to the

voters in the balmy days of early spring, they defeated it.

The hard winter does not seem to have interfered with the town's social life. Many local organizations installed new officers at the January meeting; the Knights of Columbus held a bazaar, the Junior Order of Mechanics a ladies' night and euchre. Several card clubs met weekly and there were frequent dances at Matthiessen and Red Men's Halls and at the Firthcliffe Club. These halls also presented weekly movies, where one could enjoy some of the thrillers now shown on television. N.Y.M.A. presented a carnival and mid-winter hop; the two high schools maintained their regular schedule of basketball games. The C.H.H.S. PTA held a reception for Principal and Mrs. John A. Hitzelberg. The former had gone to Florida during the Christmas vacation and returned with a new wife. C.H.S. had to close for a few days, not for bad weather, but for lack of coal.

The churches were busy with various activities. The Men's Club of the Cornwall Presbyterian Church was holding a series of films on Biblical topics; the Methodist choir was rehearsing for a concert to benefit the Girl Scouts. St. John's Church had recently installed a radio in the Parish House. The public was invited to Sunday afternoon broadcasts by the popular Rev. S. Parker Cadman. The apparatus malfunctioned on the first attempt, but thereafter the broadcasts were a regular feature, as were concerts from stations WJZ and WEAF. In those days, the purchase of a radio merited an item in the paper.

It was a sickly winter with many cases of grippe (flu) reported. The columns of the newspaper are filled with the names of the sufferers; the Colonial Tea Room, located in Matthiessen Hall, delivered broth and soup to homes where there was sickness.

When weather conditions were right, sleighriding was a popular sport. Duncan Avenue provided a long hill; ashes placed at the junction with Hudson Street prevented sleds from careening out into the main street. Another course was to start down the last hill on the Storm King Highway and coast the length of Bay View Avenue. In vain were the warnings against coasting on the main streets —dangerous to riders and pedestrians alike.

Ezra P. Thompson, walking down Mountain Road, was knocked down by a toboggan from Storm King School, to the alarm of the students, but he was not hurt. In the days before refrigerators, harvesting ice on local ponds was a necessary winter occupation. Grant Clark had a number of workmen cutting ice on Rings Pond to fill his ice house which stood on the site of the Christmas manger tableau.

From a look at the winter of 1923 it is apparent that a less complicated lifestyle resulted in fewer problems. Would anyone want to return to the "Good old Days?"

February 9, 1994

Problems of the 1920s

A glance at *The Cornwall Locals* of recent years gives an idea of some of the problems confronting the town—youth concerns; the need for school expansion and additional sports facilities, senseless vandalism, liquor and drug abuse. Public health problems include water purification and disposal of hazardous wastes. The frequent closing of the Storm King Highway is a perennial problem, as is the dissatisfaction with elected officials —the "outs" critical of the "ins" until the roles are reversed.

The concerns of the 1920s make an interesting contrast. In a town whose population was considerably less than at present, some of today's problems were then in evidence, while others were nonexistent. The need for a larger school was recognized, but postponed for years until the present school on Hudson Street was built in 1924. A few years later, the severe deficiencies in the school on Willow Avenue were corrected by a new section added in 1930.

With under twenty in the graduating classes of those years, there were obviously fewer young people to compete for after school and vacation jobs. Garages and gas stations offered work in addition to the clerking jobs in stores and shops. And it was not uncommon for teenagers to leave school for a full-time job. A college education was open to only a few high school graduates.

There were crimes, especially break-ins, but they were generally committed by a few hardened offenders. One boy stole a car and dismantled it to sell the parts—a distinctly modern touch. During the prohibition years, many of the local arrests were for the sale or manufacture of liquor, a condition which *The Local* blamed partly on those "respectable citizens who rented out dilapidated shacks. In far too many conspicuous instances wherein liquor has been sold, cocaine marketed, and gambling carried on, the rents have been paid to the gentlemen higher up who have been owners or agents of the properties in which law was violated, dangerous characters harbored, and the town endangered."

The Village Square, recently in the news, was beset by much the same problem in the 1920s: "Lounging" there was prohibited in 1925, "especially in front of the Weeks building where boys interfere with customers and litter the area." This building, later Santoros, was located on a corner of the Square, the same site which is today frequented by teenagers. Another more serious problem was vandalism at the public library, which occupied rooms in Matthiessen Hall. More than once the room was entered over a weekend despite the installation of new locks. "Library Attacked Again By Unknown Intruder," blared a headline, followed by a description of the malicious damage to books, library records and the interior. The perpetrator was suspected, but no public denunciation was ever made.

Traffic was a major problem of the 1920s. The opening of the Storm King Highway brought a constantly-growing stream of cars into the village—good news for the merchants, restaurants and lodging places, and for the garages and gas stations which proliferated along Bay View Avenue and Hudson

69

Street. But the roads, designed for the horse and buggy age, could not handle the accelerated motor traffic, and the conservative village and town officials, faced with mounting road budgets, preferred to patch and repair rather than rebuild. A large portion of the village board meetings was concerned with road and traffic matters. It was necessary to hire a full-time police officer to handle the vehicular traffic, which on holidays was practically non-stop along the main thoroughfares. Many of the secondary roads were still unpaved; a letter to the editor complained that Quaker Avenue was impassable.

The Storm King Highway was closed frequently—to the annoyance of the bus company which ran buses from Highland Falls through Cornwall to Newburgh—but it usually opened almost immediately. Despite the spring landslides and falling rocks, no one seems to have avoided using the road. There was a loud protest when artillery practice at West Point caused the highway to be closed for a number of hours in the morning.

When the Cornwall-on-Hudson School vacated the building on Idlewild Avenue, it was purchased by the Odd Fellows' Lodge which rented space to the post office. In the days before delivery, everyone had to stop at the post office for his mail. It was convenient for motorists to turn around by driving through the lot (now the library lawn), then part of the American Legion premises. The Legionnaires vowed to "take action" but the practice continued and the ruts grew muddier and deeper.

One letter to the editor, signed "Tired Citizen," complained about "the rowdy behavior of motorists at night." "Night after night," he wrote, "we are startled out of sound sleep to hear wild shouting by crazy crowds smashing through the public streets, yelling like lunatics or wild beasts."

A new emphasis on public health was apparent in the twenties. One ordinance required that all milk sold in the town come from tuberculin-free cows; and the PTAs sponsored free milk to be served daily to undernourished children—1,500 quarts were distributed in one school alone. The schools not only held annual physical examinations, but also scheduled clinics to which mothers could bring their preschoolers. Although not as serious as the cholera of the 19th century, which proved fatal in most cases, infectious diseases regularly swept through the town. In 1926 scarlet fever caused the cancellation of events at the New York Military Academy and was responsible for the death of a faculty member. Parents were urged to have their children receive smallpox vaccinations and to have them innoculated against diphtheria. And polio was always feared.

Cornwall was proud of its fine water supply which came from mountain reservoirs but, despite constant agitation, a sewer system was not installed until the 1930s, even later in some parts of town. Canterbury Creek, behind Main Street, into which seeped the effluent from nearby privies, was long recognized as an open sewer. An editorial of 1921 minced no words: "The Board of Health, if such a thing exists, should prohibit residents from throwing waste and garbage into the Canterbury brook. Or the Village Improvement Society should throw the Board of Health in the brook."

In the matter of local government, the editor led the community in an effort to oust the incumbents and replace them with more enlightened individuals. One of his many diatribes stated: "Instead of anticipating, we postpone. Instead of planning for what is sure to come we hesitate and hold back until it is too late to correct municipal errors all of which could easily have been avoided by a little courage, and a small amount of common sense." No wonder his tenure at *The Local* was brief!

October 5, 1994

The R.R.A.

Readers whose memories go back to the thirties will remember the R.R.A. The rest of you might like to learn about this unusual community endeavor whose goal was to provide culture and recreation for all.

The R.R.A.—short for Regional Rural Association—occupied a historic site along Awessema Creek, which flows through Mountainville. The land was part of an immense tract acquired by the Ketcham family in the 18th century. An early Ketcham built a grist mill on the banks of the creek —a vital component of pioneer life—and the settlement was called Ketchamtown until the coming of the railroad changed the name to Mountainville.

The Orr brothers arrived in Cornwall around the middle of the next century. William and John were both millers; they established themselves in an existing mill on Moodna Creek, near the intersection of Route 32 and Orr's Mills Road. Somewhat later, John Orr moved to Mountainville where he purchased the Ketcham mill, which now became the Mountainville Mill to distinguish it from his brother's enterprise at Orr's Mills. Both mills prospered, at first grinding the grain brought in by neighboring farmers, later handling large quantities of grain products shipped in by railroad. From John Orr, the mill passed to a newcomer, Frank C. Wessell, who lived near Cedar Lane in Cornwall and became an upstanding member of the community.

The property again emerged into prominence in the late 1920s when the mill and twelve surrounding acres came into the possession of David G. Holmes, a summer resident of Mountainville. Holmes had a dream —to convert the acres into a center for recreational and cultural enrichment: in his words, "an organization to supplement the work being done by church, school, library, lodge, scout troop, etc .... to foster physical, mental and moral health." It would duplicate, he hoped, the advantages found by the city-dweller in a multitude of urban societies. Holmes envisioned the formation of many clubs catering to the interests of all ages: athletic clubs, children's groups, current event forums, music, swimming, dramatics, Bible classes, domestic arts, and others—all meeting at the Mountainville headquarters. Being a man of means as well as a visionary, he was prepared to underwrite the project for the first few years.

During the summer of 1928, while the mill was being converted into a clubhouse, while a swimming pool was being created from the millpond, and athletic fields were under construction, Holmes started Sunday outdoor programs which soon began to attract a respectable audience. "A close-cropped meadow bounded by the brook which once turned the wheels of the Mountainville mills of John Orr is the setting of an experiment in rural community life. There on Sunday afternoon nearly 500 folk from the region to the south and west of Newburgh gathered for the Sunday program of the R.R.A."

That first summer Holmes experimented with the Sunday activities — ballgames, community singing, talks by the county Y.M.C.A. director and by the Rev. Wallace Finch, a former local pastor. One Sunday, the 22-piece Firthcliffe Band gave a concert; on another occasion, movies of the ballgames were shown. In the fall Holmes formed a large committee with representatives from every sector of the 12-mile radius included in the "R.R.A. circle"; each worker was to spread the word of the new association and secure memberships of one dollar or more. As soon as the renovations were completed, local organizations were encouraged to make use of the new facilities. A Thanksgiving costume party was held there and winter plans included a skating rink and weekly movies. By 1929 the R.R.A. was well underway. Independence Day was celebrated by sports contests, a basket dinner, a patriotic oration; in lieu of fireworks, a monstrous bonfire brought the day to a close.

The early thirties saw the full flowering of Holmes' dream. A weekly column, R.R.A. Notes, in *The Cornwall Local* kept the public abreast of the host of activities. There was something scheduled for every day of the week. A glee club met on Wednesday, a boys gym class on Friday. Miss Dorothy Paffendorf of Newburgh instructed a dancing class; there

71

was a women's forum and frequent card parties; Sunday hikes were held and the afternoon programs continued. The dramatics club produced a play in April,1930; in May the glee club and 50-member band gave their first concert, which was later broadcast from station WOKO in Beacon. A Memorial Day program was followed by others on Flag Day and Independence Day. During the summer, several of the Cornwall churches used the R.R.A. field for Sunday School picnics. A day-long event on Labor Day opened the fall season; then came an October jamboree, Halloween and Christmas festivities.

Over the next few years, the R.R.A. kept up the same frenetic pace: club meetings, parties, plays, concerts, lectures, special celebrations on the holidays. The association had been formally organized in 1929 with 12 directors and elected officers. Thomas Trolsen of Mountainville served as president for several terms. By 1936 he was making an urgent appeal for community support—from a peak membership of nine hundred, the goal was now reduced to four hundred. With Holmes no longer funding the R.R.A., it gradually declined.

In 1943 the property was taken over by the American Youth Hostels; then in 1946, it was purchased by the Black Rock Fish and Game Club, a sportsmen's group which had been in existence for many years. Now, almost fifty years later, the site is still the headquarters of the club. The next time you pass that way, think of the old mill in its first pastoral setting and of its later conversion into a Utopian experiment.

August 31,1993

Cornwall in 1930

This section on community changes ends with a survey of 1930. Some of the highlights of that year can be said to encompass both nostalgia and progress.

That winter Fred Leach of Firthcliffe held a dinner to commemorate the forty-sixth anniversary of his arrival in the United States. He had started work at the British plant of the Firth Carpet Company in 1869 and had continued his affiliation at the branch in Cornwall—an aggregate of sixty-one years! Present at the dinner were four other veteran workers: James H. Aspinall, Fred Booth, Harry W. Briggs and George H.C. Hole, all of whom had started in the parent company.

Another retrospective occasion—the Hundredth Anniversary of the Highland Engine Company—celebrated by a banquet at the Storm King Arms, open house at the banner-draped fire house and a parade in which the company was joined by its fellow firemen from the Storm King Engine Company.

And in 1930, twelve years after the 1918 Armistice, a war memorial is finally set up in the Friends Cemetery, bearing the inscription: "In Memory of Our Dead Heroes, Soldiers, Sailors, Marines and Nurses of All Wars, U.S.A."

The most visible signs of progress are two important buildings: an annex more than doubles the size of the Cornwall High School on Willow Avenue and the new Cornwall Hospital is rising on a slope to the south of the town's business district. Less tangible but significant progress can be found in the field of public health. A Visiting Nurse Society exists for the sole purpose of sponsoring a nurse who makes regular visits to the infirm and assists the town physicians when needed. In a more health-conscious era, school clinics are routine—for immunization shots, physicals and "well-baby" clinics. The most aggravating form of progress that year is the widening and resurfacing of Cornwall's main thoroughfares. The work lasts for many months during which detours, mud, dust, ruts, potholes and ripped-up sidewalks make getting around town a nightmare.

When we compare 1930 with 1896, many

changes are apparent in the fabric of daily life. Garages and gas stations take the place of blacksmith shops and livery stables. According to *The Local*, there are at least a dozen "motor shops" and gas stations between the Storm King Highway and the Academy Avenue bridge.

The mammoth hotels of the past century have disappeared and most of the summer boarding houses are now concentrated along Angola Road and in Mountainville. Fund raising is a never ceasing necessity, but the purposes and activities have changed. The American Legion, a post-war organization, and its auxiliary have pledged an ambulance for the new hospital, an effort requiring many benefits, such as a fair, a roast beef dinner (tickets 75¢ and 40¢), and a showing of the Eddie Cantor film "Whoopee" at the N.Y.M.A. chapel.

The most popular fund-raisers are amateur theatricals and card parties, with an occasional concert and silver tea. St. Thomas Dramatic Circle, a long-established group, is now faced with competition from the West Point Players, the Cornwall Dramatic Club with Edward C. Krug as director, and the plays produced by Clinton Noe. Almost every month one can find announcements of a play, usually a comedy, presented by one of the groups.

As some of the older fraternal organizations disbanded, new associations take their place. The Cornwall Garden Club meets each month to hear papers on horticultural topics by its members and to plan flower shows—two were held that year in the old Union Hotel on Main Street (later Hey's Store). The R.R.A. is the town's largest organization with a membership over eight hundred. So much is taking place at its Mountainville headquarters that *The Local* never lacks a news item. A July headline: "Fourth of July Program Pleases Throng at R.R.A. Day of Sports is Followed by Picnic Supper and Band and Glee Club Concerts." The "throng" is estimated at over a thousand.

It would take many words to describe the changes in the Cornwall schools between 1896 and 1930. During this period the two largest districts have been forced by increasing enrollments to build new schools—on Hudson Street (C.H.H.S.) and Willow Avenue (C.H.S.) Both the subject matter and the extra-curricular activities have expanded notably in sports; tennis, soccer and swim meets are popular along with the traditional basketball and baseball. With bus transportation available, it is possible for the schools to compete in county sports' leagues. The senior class travels to Washington, D.C. during the Easter vacation; much energy goes into raising money for this annual excursion—cake sales, dances, school-wide entertainments, concerts and plays.

A different lifestyle now places more emphasis on recreation. The sports news increases in volume to include both school games and accounts of the town baseball leagues. The Twilight and City Leagues, sponsored by the Cornwall-on-Hudson Athletic Association, compete with the Firthcliffe and other town clubs. Miniature golf is a new fad. August 22nd: "Rapid progress is being made on the miniature golf course which is being installed on the property in front of Rings Pond." Long before the creation of the Town Hall Park, this section is being improved, the grounds landscaped, the pool drained and cleaned so it can be used for swimming, the former ice house converted into dressing rooms. Whether all of these plans materialized is not mentioned, but the golf course is evidently a success, for several other miniature courses sprout all over town.

The year 1930 does not pass without its share of problems. Two fires occur in April: Schwab's Garage (on the site of the Hudson Street post office) is destroyed by a fire that threatens several adjacent buildings, and the Stillman boathouse at the Landing burns down. Later in the year another fire in a tenement called "The Beehive," endangers the west side of Main Street. Schwab puts up a new garage of cinder blocks, repairs are made to "The Beehive" but the boathouse is not rebuilt. A violent storm in July damages many old trees along the village streets.

Among the chief events of the year are the installation of Rev. Robert Gay as rector of St. John's Episcopal Church, the laying of the hospital cornerstone as part of the Memorial Day observance, a costume ball for two hundred guests held by Richard Scandrett, the new owner of the Van Duzer house on Pleasant Hill Road. On the church scene are an Evangelistic Conference by the Baptists, a two-week mission at St. Thomas Church, the Methodist fair and supper at the Masonic Temple, and the annual chicken supper at the A.M.E. Zion Church on Main Street. The Sixth Annual Dog Show at Kenridge Farm attracts thousands of visitors to an event that grows larger each year.

Central Hudson, which supplies Cornwall with electricity now plans to lay gas mains. From cooking by coal range, to electric and gas stoves, electric refrigerators and washing machines—the housewife's lot is considerably less burdensome from that of her mother's.

Many properties have a garage for the family car and a radio in the living room is no longer a novelty. Now that "talkies" have superseded the silent movies, Cornwallites have to patronize the movie theaters in Newburgh until 1935, when the Storm King Theatre opens in Cornwall.

No major crime disturbs the town in 1930; aside from coping with traffic, the police officer's chief preoccupation is to work with the state troopers in liquor raids —prohibition is still in effect. The Depression is being felt in Cornwall; the King's Daughters whose charitable work has hitherto been confined to Thanksgiving baskets for the poor, suddenly finds its funds depleted by increasing demands—it has spent over five hundred dollars in aid to the needy. The group makes an unprecedented appearance at a well-attended basketball game in order to take up a collection.

The Cornwall Local has acquired a new editor, Raymond S. Preston, a new office (in a building on his Hasbrouck Avenue property) and a new format of eight columns instead of six. In addition to the town and regional news, there are new features: serial stories for adults and children, fashions and recipes, comics, and a page of world and national news in photographs. "Devoted to Village Improvement and Community Progress," proclaims the masthead; the yearly subscription rate is now two dollars.

PEOPLE

It has been very difficult to select a few Cornwallites to represent the early 20th century. Each reader with a knowledge of the period will have a different choice. Here is my list: two influential businessmen, father and son, who were also respected community leaders; a philanthropist whose generosity enriched the town to an unusual degree; a physician whose flare for public speaking led to a role as the town's unofficial master of ceremonies; a school superintendent with a distinguished military career and a strong interest in public affairs; and a man of humble birth whose life embodied service to his country and to his hometown, especially the youth.

There are no women on the list, but the reader has found their accomplishments in many of the articles as they edit an early newspaper, beautify the town, save the Old Homestead, fight for Equal Suffrage, contribute to the war effort and raise money for countless good works.

The Tafts

When Charles H. Mead, the senior partner of Mead and Taft Company, died in 1905, his obituary summed up the early history of the firm: the 1853 partnership of Mead and Daniel Taft and the reorganization in 1866 when Thomas Taft replaced his father. Of this relationship, lasting almost forty years, the obituary commented that the two men "never exchanged an unpleasant or impatient word with one another"; differences were thrashed out until a mutually satisfactory solution was reached.

Thomas Taft was to outlive his partner by fifteen years. He was born in 1840, the oldest son of Daniel and Emeline Taft, and was educated at the Alfred C. Roe Collegiate School in Cornwall where he studied surveying. At the outbreak of the Civil War, he enlisted in the county's 124th Regiment, the Orange Blossoms. Wounded at Gettysburg, he was captured and detained for a time in the infamous Libby prison. After a furlough, he returned to service until the end of the war, rising to the rank of captain. Back from the war, Taft worked for a brief period in the wholesale business in New York City, then returned to Cornwall to join Mead and Taft which then employed a work force of about twenty which increased to five hundred when the firm was at its peak.

In 1919 Mr. Taft's health began to fail, but he persisted in attending to business; his final estimate won the contract to build the Saint Elizabeth Chapel at Eagle Valley, New York. He died the following winter, in February, 1920.

For over half a century, Thomas Taft—Captain Taft many called him in recognition of his Civil War service—had been "a large part of the life of Cornwall." Not only head of the firm which gave employment to so many local people, he was the first mayor of the Village of Cornwall after its incorporation in 1884, serving four terms in all.[1] He organized the Cornwall Electric Lighting and Power Company to supply the town with electricity and telephones. He was responsible for bringing the Ontario and Western Railroad Coal

---

1   He served from 1885-89 and 1891-95.

Dock to the town, thereby adding to the local economy. He was a strong temperance man, a pillar of the Cornwall Presbyterian Church, perennial chairman of drives for worthy causes—no man was better known in the community. Despite bad weather, three hundred people attended his funeral; business places closed and village flags flew at half staff.

Thomas K. Taft, the captain's son, now took over at Mead and Taft. A graduate of Columbia University with a degree in Mining Engineering, he worked for eight years at a mine in Telluride, Colorado. *The Local* records his occasional visits to the East and his marriage in 1913 to Miss Beulah G. Mc Glinch of Telluride. The couple spent the winter of 1914 in Cornwall; a few years later Taft gave up his mining career to help his father at the family plant. And he remained at the helm through the company's slow decline— through the depression, through the war years when the factory was leased to a ship building company and a fire in 1944 deccimated the plant. Mead and Taft rebuilt for the third time, and shared its premises with another business. But times had changed; modern developers could outbid the older firm and there was no longer a market for the fine millwork which had been the hallmark of an older generation of carpenters. When Con Ed leveled Cornwall Landing in preparation for its proposed stor-age plant at Storm King Mountain, the old Mead and Taft factory met the same fate as the neighboring structures.

Thomas K. Taft died in 1978 at age ninety-six. He had succeeded his father as president of Mead and Taft and like his father, he was an active participant in civic and cultural affairs, serving on the Board of Directors or as a Trustee of the Newburgh and Cornwall hospitals, the historical society in Newburgh, the Cornwall bank, the county Boy Scout, Salvation Army and YMCA committees.

"Many of Cornwall's present older residences stand as a lasting tribute to the workmanship of Mead and Taft Co.," stated his obituary. One of these is the family home on River Avenue which evolved from a small house enlarged by Daniel Taft and his son, then was drastically altered by the second Thomas who, in 1928, moved a portion of the house across the street and remodeled the remaining section.

After his wife's death in 1940, Taft lived on in his home, but traveled widely and kept in touch with his three children. He is remembered as a very youthful senior citizen with a zest for life, a twinkle in his eye, and a phenomenal memory of the past. The public library is fortunate to possess a number of tapes which preserve his meticulous account of Cornwall history.

General Milton F. Davis

In its 106-year history, the New York Military Academy has had a number of administrators, each with his own unique qualifications. The subject of this article is General Milton F. Davis. Although his tenure (1922-1936) was not as long as other superintendents, his years at the school extended over nearly thirty years. And he brought to the job the experience of a long military career as well as outstanding abilities.

Milton Fenimore Davis was born in Minnesota in 1864. After attending the University of Oregon for two years, he received an appointment to the U.S. Military Academy at West Point, from which institution he graduated in 1890. With a commission of second lieutenant in the U.S. Cavalry, he was stationed at Fort Walla Walla, Washington, then at the Presidio in San Francisco. "During this time the troops spent the summers in the National Parks, and Davis surveyed and mapped the entire Sierra Forest Reserve... and explored the Grand Canyon... from northern Arizona to the Gulf of California." After he made the first ascent of a 12,000-foot peak in the High Sierras, it was named Mount Davis at the recommendation of his friend, John Muir.

Davis' next tour of duty was in Cuba and the Philippine Islands where he saw service in the Spanish-American War. From 1903-1907, he was Adjutant General and Chief of Staff to the Commanding General in the Philippines, followed by two years as Aide to the Chief of Staff in Washington, D.C.

Forced by a heart ailment to retire from active service, Davis joined the N.Y.M.A. staff in 1909 as Professor of Military Science and Tactics, and Commandant. Here his qualities of organizational ability, good judgment, patience, resourcefulness and industry were invaluable. He had been only a few months at N.Y.M.A. when a raging fire in January 1910, destroyed the main school building, formerly a large, rambling summer hotel. The problems of housing the cadets in temporary quarters and the organizing of a stock company to provide the funding to rebuild required extraordinary exertions from everyone on the staff.

When America entered the first World War in 1917, Davis was recalled to active service, assigned to the Signal Corps, then to the new U.S. Air Service where he was Chief of Training. Cornwall received a thrill when his De Haviland war plane landed on the N.Y.M.A. parade ground. After the war he returned to the school, retired as a Lieutenant Colonel, then commissioned a Colonel and later a Brigadier General in the U.S. Air Corps Reserve. In 1923 he was awarded the Distinguished Service Medal.

With the retirement that year of N.Y.M.A. Superintendent Sebastian C. Jones, General Davis was appointed to the post. *The Cornwall Locals* record the prosperous decades of the 1920s and 1930s. The school acquired adjacent property on which new buildings, including stables, were located. An addition to the Academic Building contained an impressive chapel. The West Barracks was built, also a gym, swimming pool, and a home for the Davis family. The school enrollment soared, according to *The Local*, and the cadets won accolades for athletic prowess and for the school publication, *The Ramble;* and N.Y. M.A. passed its routine government inspections with commendation.

The social events became more brilliant; the concerts, lectures and other programs in the chapel more frequent. Some of the school's success was doubtless due to the ability and experience of the incumbent administrator, General Davis.

From his first years at N.Y.M.A., Davis took an interest in Cornwall. For a time the family lived in the village, in the "Ryckman Place" on River Avenue, and they made many friends in the community. Davis used to join a fall hunting party to the Catskills; one year he went to Nova Scotia. It is to his credit that, holding memberships in national organizations, he nevertheless promoted the groups' activities at the local level. As a member of the National Boy Scout Council, he supported scouting in Cornwall and headed the Orange County committee. While belonging to the U.S. Chamber of Commerce, he was president of the Hudson Valley Chamber and active in the Cornwall unit. He was a founding member of the Cornwall American Legion post and its first president. He served for years as a director of the Cornwall National Bank, and he was a frequent speaker at community affairs.

During the Davis superintendency, Cornwall was welcome to use the school facilities: the Hudson Highlands Art Association held its shows in the gym as did the Cornwall Garden Club; "Pop" Tibbitts staged a large convention at N.Y.M.A., and dinners in the Mess Hall for community events were not uncommon.

In 1936 General Davis resigned as superintendent and was given the title of N.Y.M.A. president. His death came two years later, in May 1938; after the funeral services in the Davis Chapel, he was interred at West Point. He was survived by his wife Bessie, a son and two daughters. A son-in-law, Captain Frank Pattillo, succeeded him as N.Y.M.A. superintendent to begin a new era at the school.

July 26, 1995

Dr. Ralph Waldo Thompson

No one of the period had his name more frequently in the newspaper than Ralph Waldo Thompson, a fact which he did nothing to prevent. This colorful figure came to Cornwall in 1908 to take over the medical practice of Dr. David H. Chandler who had died earlier in the year. An item from *The Local* of August 27th states that Mrs. Chandler had rented her home to Dr. Thompson, a homeopathic physician like his predecessor. The house, which he later bought, stands on Hudson Street across from the entrance to the Little League fields.

Born in Albany in 1876 and orphaned at an early age, Dr. Thompson was forced to work his way through college. After graduating from Troy Conference Academy at Poultney, Vermont, in 1889, he earned the tuition for Middlebury College by preaching, and graduated from that institution in 1903, after which he took a post graduate course at Drew Seminary. Then, deciding on a medical career, he studied at the New York Medical College from which he graduated in 1908 and hung out his shingle in Cornwall.

Presumably, Dr. Thompson soon built up a practice among the townspeople; he is mentioned as attending a sick patient or being called to the scene of an accident. But a flair for public speaking, acquired from his training for the ministry, led him to participate in so many fraternal and civic organizations that more was reported about this aspect of his life than on his professional activities. He was a great joiner— one article in *The Local* takes thirty lines to list all of his affiliations: several Masonic groups including the local lodge, the Mountainville Grange, a worthy patron and assistant grand lecturer of the Eastern Star lodge, a high official in the Red Men's Order. In 1912 Dr. Thompson was busy teaching first aid to the Boy Scouts; next he was involved in the formation of a Rifle Club. He was elected master of the Jerusalem Temple Lodge in 1915, then became a district deputy Grand Master which entailed visitations to other lodges in the area. In 1919 he helped organize the Cornwall Order of Eastern Stars and served as its patron for the first ten years and for two later terms. He joined the Waoroneck Tribe of Red Men and rose through the ranks to be installed as the Great Sachem of New York State. He must have taken great pleasure in the regalia and rites of these fraternal organizations, but even more pleasing were the opportunities to address a group or to serve as toastmaster.

If this were not enough, Dr. Thompson was a trustee of the Cornwall Methodist Church, whose pulpit he was happy to fill when the minister was on vacation. As trustee of the Cornwall High School Board of Education, he was instrumental, naturally, in starting a prize speaking contest. His name generally appeared as a member of the town Memorial Day Committee and he sponsored a Memorial Day Appropriation Bill in the state legislature permitting towns to designate funds for this patriotic observance.

Dr. Thompson also joined the local medical societies, was president of the Odell Tuberculosis Sanitarium in Newburgh, and in 1918 he owned for a brief period the Cornwall Sanitarium on the site of the future elementary school on Hudson Street.

In 1918 he was appointed the Town Health Officer, a post he held for over thirty years. A growing awareness of public health during those years led to the testing of the dairy herds which supplied the town's milk supply, to school clinics for diphtheria and smallpox shots, and the medical examination of preschool children. Dr. Thompson was given credit for establishing these modern procedures in Cornwall and for sponsoring speakers on public health topics, himself included.

After a four-year term as Village Health Officer (1924-1928), Dr. Thompson was not re-appointed because of "policy differences" with the Village Board. His letter of congratulation to his successor, a Highland Falls physician, points out that the latter does not possess the necessary qualifications, a fact later proven to be incorrect.

In 1923 the readers of *The Local* learned that Dr. Thompson had in his office the largest x-ray machine in the Hudson Valley, costing over $1,800; and he was treating tuberculosis by x-ray "with great success." The article explained that "Dr. Thompson also has a high

78

frequency attachment... used principally in treating neuritis, equalizing circulation, goiter, high blood pressure, and hardening of the arteries, all without pain or discomfort." When the Cornwall Hospital opened in 1931, Dr. Thompson became the radiologist.

It was his connection with the Improved Order of Red Men which gave Dr. Thompson the most publicity. He probably joined the Waoroneck Lodge soon after coming to Cornwall; he entered the Great Council in 1919; and rose from Great Junior Sagamore to Great Senior Sagamore and in 1926 to Great Sachem of the state. This exalted post he filled with "marked efficiency," making over sixty visitations throughout New England and the Middle Atlantic States. When did he find time to use his expensive x-ray machine?

He arranged to have many of his speeches, also his articles for the Red Men's publication reprinted in *The Local.* One of them elaborates on his notion that the dignity of the Red Men Deputies would be enhanced by the wearing of dress suits. Another discusses what the Red Men's Lodge means to a member—a club, a bond of brotherhood, a clique, or "a service chain." Another piece is entitled "The Ships We Fly" —Lindbergh had just made his solo flight across the Atlantic —here he alludes to Censorship, Companionship and Friendship. When his term as Great Sachem expired, *The Local* featured a picture of Dr. Thompson on the front page with the text of the farewell address he delivered to the brethren at Watkins Glen. As he grew older, Dr. Thompson retired from some of these fraternal duties, but in 1946 he served as president of the Orange County Medical Society and, at the time of his death in January 1948, he was still on the staff of the Cornwall Hospital.

The Hometown Movie of 1929 depicts Dr. Thompson in one of the scenes. To oblige the photographer, he rounded up a number of fellow Red Men who, in full regalia, enacted "authentic" Indian rites in a wooded glade: tomahawking a rotund member who was tied to the stake, and running the gauntlet. He obviously had no compunction about having these silly antics preserved for posterity!

June 21, 1995

Leo A. Fanning

Almost everyone is familiar with the pictures of Leo Fanning which have appeared in *The Cornwall Local* during the past decades—a serious, yet friendly face, radiating good humor and contentment. But few would recognize the young World War I soldier pictured in the newspaper of January 24, 1918 when PFC Fanning, age 21, was driving an ambulance in France.

America entered the war in April 1917; Leo enlisted two months later, but was not called to active service until the following November when he joined the Third Evacuation Hospital Unit. By the beginning of the new year (1918), so many Cornwallites were in the armed forces that the newspaper started a front-page column entitled "Cornwall Men in the U.S. Service." Families of servicemen were invited to furnish photos and biographical data, and were also encouraged to buy extra copies of the paper when the article appeared.

Beneath Leo's picture is a short piece stating that he was the second son of Michael Fanning, was educated at the Cornwall-on-Hudson school, after which "he attended the Y.M.C.A. training school for a time, where he was a member of the Hospital Corps and received practical instruction which will be of great help in the new life he has taken up." The article continues: "He is well known throughout Orange county as an athlete and has won many medals."

Growing up within a stone's throw of the river, Leo enjoyed boating and swimming with his friends, and skating when the river was frozen over. As a teenager he joined the Garden Athletic Club started by Miss Beatrice Abbott. The members tended garden plots at the Abbott estate on Clark Avenue and sold the produce to obtain funds for sports equipment.

79

Later, under Miss Abbott's guidance, the group built and maintained the gym which became a center for athletics, dances and other activities.

Leo had to leave school to help support his family. As early as 1911, he was working as a clerk at the Cornwall Grocery Store; at the time of his enlistment he was driving for Mead and Taft Company. Even to a fellow used to hard work, life in the Ambulance Corps was hectic.

"Dear Mother," wrote Leo on August 20, 1918, "Just at present I am pushed for all I am worth. I have sometimes driven for two days and a night without sleep and it sure does get a fellow. Sometimes I make a bed in the ambulance." He went on to describe a trip taken recently with beautiful scenery reminding him of Cornwall. "Whenever I cart wounded, I sure do keep a lookout for any boys I might know from home." Another letter written shortly after the Armistice reads: "It is just one year tonight that the K. of C. gave us boys the big time [This was a send-off by the Cornwall Knights of Columbus Council]. Just one year of army life. I do not know how many more months we will be over here ... it will not seem long before we are jumping off the train when the conductor calls out 'Cornwall, Cornwall'."

As a senior citizen, half a century later, Leo enjoyed reminiscing and was frequently interviewed. He would relate his war experiences, his return to civilian life in 1919, and his marriage in 1921 to Anna Miller. He took a job with the Bear Mountain police; one of the duties was to patrol— sometimes on foot — the newly-opened Storm King Highway. In 1923 he was appointed police chief of Cornwall-on-Hudson; and given a uniform, a motorcycle, a budget of three thousand dollars, and an annual salary of about $1,500. For a time his beat covered Canterbury and Firthcliffe as well as the lower village. The Hometown Movie of 1929 has a fine picture of Police Chief Fanning astride his motorcycle, a handsome figure and one to command respect. Whenever the film was shown in the 1970s and 1980s, Leo was sure to be present, and would sit through all of the showings to savor this memory of the past. He also found

time to coach a basketball team, head a Boy Scout troop, join the Storm King Engine Company and the American Legion. He took part in minstrel shows, singing Irish songs or playing the harmonica.

In 1930 he changed jobs, becoming postmaster of Cornwall-on-Hudson, a position he held until retiring in 1956. Both as policeman and postmaster, Leo came into contact with the public and was a familiar and well-liked figure.

When World War II began, Leo was commander of the Cornwall American Legion Post. He formed a home guard of boys and older men—the Legion Battalion— which he trained in the N.Y.M.A. gym. After Pearl Harbor, he helped form civil defense units and establish an airplane lookout post which was manned round the clock.

In later years, Leo continued to be active in civic and religious affairs. He was a member of the committee which reconstructed the village bandstand—he had once played in the original band. Memorial Day was a special occasion to Leo, and he came to be identified with the holiday, marching in the parade and often acting as marshal. In January 1986, Leo celebrated his nintieth birthday and received greetings from President Reagan and Governor Cuomo; also a special resolution from the State Assembly and a reception by the Legion post at which he received congratulations from a host of townspeople. Three years later, Leo died, on May 27, 1989, and was eulogized a few days afterward on Memorial Day. "A wreath and folded American flag borne on a car in the ... parade were a reminder that the physical presence of Leo Fanning was gone. But in the banners, martial music, flowers, salutes and speeches marking Memorial Day 1989, his spirit lived."

And this year came another "special moment"—the dedication of a monument "to mark the community's respect for one of its finest." Take time to stop at the Village Square—now named "Fanning Square" to read the inscription, admire the bas relief portrait of Leo, and the tasteful planting surrounding the stone.

June 21, 1995

Dr. Ernest G. Stillman

In addition to being a philanthropist, as exemplified by his gift of The Cornwall Hospital and numerous other benefactions, what sort of person was Dr. Stillman? Three sources help to supply the answer. From biographical volumes come the basic data: Ernest Goodrich Stillman, born in 1884, son of banker James Stillman; educated at Groton, graduated from Harvard in 1907 and from Columbia Medical School in 1913; associated with Rockefeller Institute from 1915 until 1949 (the year of his death) where he specialized in pneumonia and influenza research; served in the Medical Corps during World War I; married Mildred Whitney in 1911 and had six children; chief interests: preservation of the "natural beauties" of the Hudson Highlands, the study of forestry, and fire-fighting.

The Cornwall Local provides the details to round out these basic facts. From July 14, 1898: "Mr. James Stillman has made preparations to celebrate the 14th birthday of his youngest son, Ernest, at his country home this evening. A magnificent display of fireworks will be a feature of the occasion." His father had built a house (now Jogue's Retreat) at the top of Duncan Avenue; his grandmother and aunts lived nearby in the house now known as The Grail. In 1903 young Stillman gave a dance for his friends in the family boathouse at Cornwall Landing (near the present Yacht Club). That summer he and his brother had a two-oared shell on the river, and were instructed perhaps by Dan Ward, a relative of the famous Ward Brothers[2].

On his return East from his marriage in San Francisco, Stillman, already involved with the local fire companies, hosted a chowder supper for the Storm King Engine Company as was the custom for newly-married members. In 1916 he was having a house built on the mountain, a simple colonial-style farmhouse, far less elegant than his father's spacious mansion. The development of Stillwood Farm followed, with the construction of barns and other outbuildings, the laying out of meadows and gardens, and the hiring of workmen to run the farm.

Although he maintained a home in the city, Cornwall was close to Dr. Stillman's heart —it would be impossible to list all of his contributions to the community. In 1919, to combat the effects of the post-war recession, he started the Allied Industries, the name later changed to the Cornwall Industrial Association. This organization comprised several departments, one of which was *The Local*, then published under the name of *The Cornwall Press.* The corporation headquarters was located in the long one-story building at the corner of Main Street and Willow Avenue. A few years later another building was erected on Shore Road which ultimately became The Cornwall Press, "a busy book manufacturing concern." The newspaper makes frequent reference to this business— noting the employees, a list of the books published there and the activities of the men's and women's basketball teams formed by the employees. All together these various enterprises gave work to a sizable number of local people.

Another contribution of a different sort was the German cannon from World War I which stands in the small park across from the Town Hall. Through the auspices of Dr. Stillman, it was presented to Cornwall by the government of France. Among Dr. Stillman's many benefactions to Harvard, his alma mater, that of Black Rock Forest, a large tract of mountain land lying partially within the town, is of most immediate interest to Cornwall. Here he co-operated with the university over a long period as "sponsor of a research project in hardwood silviculture." After his death, the forest was left to Harvard with a large endowment to help maintain it. It is currently owned by a consortium of educational institutions and used both for research and as an outdoor laboratory for large numbers of students.

Fire-fighting was one of Dr. Stillman's longtime hobbies and he had affiliations with both Storm King and Highland Engine Companies. He attended their functions whenever

---

2   Cornwall's champion oarsmen won fame at the International Regatta, at Saratoga on September 11, 1876.

he was in town and delighted in surprising them with donations ranging from antique memorabilia to the latest in fire-fighting apparatus. As chief of the Cornwall Fire Department in 1922, he led the firemen at a convention parade in Beacon; on this occasion he fell and injured his leg.

Dr. Stillman served for years as a trustee of Storm King School to which he donated substantially in defraying the deficits and in funding a new infirmary. One year he addressed the Men's Club of the Cornwall Presbyterian Church, describing his medical research in such lucid terms, according to one listener, that even a schoolchild could have understood it.

Of the people in Cornwall who remember Dr. Stillman, each has a different story to relate. One recalls his sense of humor and his love of pranks; another his love of the out-of-doors, especially his beloved forest; another has a story about his predilection for doing good by stealth. The postmistress at Cornwall Landing, the conductors on the trains, the workmen at Stillwood Farm and Black Rock Forest (including the rattlesnake experts), the shopkeepers and tradesmen, his fellow firemen—all were his friends. Don't be misled by the stiff portrait in the reception room at the hospital—behind the formal pose was a warm, compassionate, perceptive man.

My parents were good friends of Dr. Stillman; my mother who used to write short poems, some of which appeared in *The Local*, was inspired to compose two tributes to this uncommon man.

CORNWALL HOSPTTAL
(To E.G.S.)

His Norfolk jacket quite threadbare
And trousers frayed from lack of care,
An old misshapen brown felt hat,
Shoes scuffed and scarred, but what of that?
His interest in affairs and men
Like the five talents grew to ten.
Where'er he lived, where'er he went,
Men spoke the word, "Benevolent."

In our own town he bought some ground,
He cleared the land, then paced it round
And marked the spot with his flat foot
Just where the building must be put.
"Save the big oak — a noble tree,"
He said, — and well, we all can see
The institution he began. -
This "lengthened shadow of one man."

He quoted Beaconsfield to me:
How men might form community,
but stressed this part of the quotation:
"*Institutions* create nations."

BLACK ROCK FOREST
(To E.G.S.)

No obelisk of polished stone
No pyramid, or marble tomb,
No rough-hewn slab, no monument
Marks where your scattered ashes lie,
Here life abounds, and does not die.

Beneath the lush, moist forest floor
A future wealth is all secure
Your special care, your one intent
That where your scattered ashes lie,
Life should go on and never die.

How fortunate we natives are
That your far-vision did preserve
This vast encircling wilderness
Where, though your ashes scattered lie
Life will recur, and never die.

No monument is needed here:
Green trees or branches winterbare
In every season will profess
That where your scattered ashes lie
Life is assured and will not die.

Laura B. Dempsey
May 11, 1994

BIBLIOGRAPHY

The Cornwall Newspapers provided the source for most of the articles:
> *The Cornwall Reflector, The Reflector of Cornwall,*
> *The Cornwall Times, The Local-Press, Cornwall Press,*
> *The Cornwall Press, The Cornwall Local.*

Beach, Lewis. *Cornwall*. Newburgh, N.Y.: E.M. Ruttenber & Sons, 1873.

Cornwall Business directories of the late 19th century.

Cornwall Hospital Brochure, undated.

Cornwall Hospital, First and Second Annual Reports.

Cornwall Industrial Corporation Brochure, undated.

Handy Guide to the Hudson River and the Catskill Mountains. The Hudson-Fulton
> Celebration edition, New York: Rand McNally & Co., 1911.

Lathrop, J.M. *Atlas of Orange County, N.Y.* Philadelphia: A.H. Mueller & Co.,
> 1903.

Orange County Deeds. Office of the County Clerk, Goshen, N.Y.

Schiff, Martha, ed. "In Celebration Cornwall 200 Years": *The Cornwall Local,*
> News of the Highlands, Inc., 1976.

ACKNOWLEDGMENTS

I am grateful to the Friends of the Cornwall Public Library for underwriting this book; to the Library for permission to reproduce the painting by Robert 0. Chadeayne, and for the unfailing patience and helpfulness of the staff; to *The Cornwall Local* for permission to reprint the articles from the newspaper and for the cheerful cooperation of its staff. I am indebted to Colette C. Fulton for assistance with the newspaper index, to James I. O'Neill who established the Library's slide collection, to Michael Nelson for the illustrations, and to Cathy Kelly for proofreading. I am grateful to Virginia Norrey for the map of Cornwall and to Maria Miller for her advice on the book design.

As for the scores of townspeople who have eagerly shared their own knowledge of the past, I will use the device of Cornwall's first historian Lewis Beach who wrote: "To avoid invidious distinctions ... mention of particular names is forborne." The list would be very long!

INDEX